GENDER ISSUES IN ETHNOGRAPHY, 2nd Edition

CAROL A. B. WARREN
JENNIFER KAY HACKNEY

Qualitative Research Methods
Volume 9

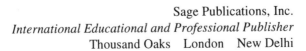
Sage Publications, Inc.
International Educational and Professional Publisher
Thousand Oaks   London   New Delhi

For information:

Sage Publications, Inc.
2455 Teller Road
Thousand Oaks, California 91320
E-mail: order@sagepub.com

Sage Publications Ltd.
6 Bonhill Street
London EC2A 4PU
United Kingdom

Sage Publications India Pvt. Ltd.
M-32 Market
Greater Kailash I
New Delhi 110 048 India

Printed in the United States of America

Library of Congress Cataloging-in-Publication Data

Warren, Carol A. B., 1944–
    Gender issues in ethnography, 2nd edition / by Carol A. B. Warren, Jennifer Kay Hackney. — 2nd ed.
        p. cm. — (Qualitative research methods; v. 9)
    Includes bibliographical references.
    ISBN 0-7619-1716-0 (cloth: alk. paper) — ISBN 0-7619-1717-9 (pbk.: alk. paper)
    1. Social sciences—Field work. 2. Anthropology—Field work. 3. Sociology—Field work. 4. Sex differences. I. Hackney, Jennifer Kay. II. Title. III. Series.
    H62 .W283 2000
    300´.7´2—dc21   99-050783

00   01   02   03   04   05   06   7   6   5   4   3   2   1

Acquiring Editor:	C. Deborah Laughton
Editorial Assistant:	Eileen Carr
Production Editor:	Diana E. Axelsen
Editorial Assistant:	Victoria Cheng
Typesetter:	Tina Hill

When citing a university paper, please use the proper form. Remember to cite the Sage University Paper series title and include the paper number. One of the following formats can be adapted (depending on the style manual used):

(1) WARREN, C. (2000). *Gender Issues in Ethnography, 2nd Edition.* Sage University Papers Series on Qualitative Research Methods, Vol. 9. Thousand Oaks, CA: Sage.

OR

(2) Warren, C. (2000). *Gender Issues in Ethnography, 2nd Edition.* (Sage University Papers Series on Qualitative Research Methods, Vol. 9). Thousand Oaks, CA: Sage.

CONTENTS

To Kathi, Kay, John, and Tim

SERIES EDITORS' INTRODUCTION

Fieldworkers would like to think that whatever they see, hear, and write up as a result of their research experience in a particular setting is what any other similarly trained and situated fieldworker would also see, hear and write up. While there might be modest differences of style and focus, whatever strikes one fieldworker as significant would surely strike another. Or so it is thought. This is an ethnographic conceit and, to a certain extent, it has kept the enterprise going for the past 60 or 70 years. Such a conceit has had its day, however. Increasingly, its practitioners regard fieldwork as a highly and almost hauntingly personal method for which no programmatic guides can be written.

Carol A. B. Warren and Jennifer Kay Hackney take up these issues in the second edition of Volume 9 of the Sage **Qualitative Research Methods Series** by focusing on the ways in which gender is experienced in the field—both on the part of researchers and on the part of those researched. Moreover, the authors show that *in situ* social research, as the polished (and written) product of a variety of field research techniques, cannot be understood by writers or readers without explicitly taking into account how gender—and the broader field of power relations in society—influences both fieldwork relations and the production of research reports. Since gender is a key organizing device in all cultures—a device that Warren and Hackney treat as both essential and negotiated in and across social relations—researchers must be continually aware of the gender impressions they are more or less giving off and taking in while in the field. And, as they so carefully suggest, this is no easy matter and cuts to the very core of qualitative field studies.

Gender Issues in Field Research draws on both anthropological and sociological examples to mark and illustrate its points. Studies of urban communities, educational settings, work organizations, and communication processes are examined in light of the role gender specifically and power generally plays in their realization. Crucial to the monograph are the various ways particular researchers in particular situations have attempted to manage and, in some cases, modify the opportunities and constraints posed by gender. In this second edition, Warren and Hackney look extensively at the interview situation as an increasingly common stage on which gender performances are enacted. The lessons here are idiosyncratic to be sure but no less important as a result. Certainly they point to the fact that gender matters in virtually all aspects of social research.

How it matters is of course the crucial question facing fieldworkers. It is a question that can be usefully addressed from many perspectives, and several promising ones are suggesting the book. But, readers beware. This is not a book about how to minimize the role gender plays in social research or how to use gender to further certain research agendas. It is first and foremost a book about how gender operates everywhere and always, but in particular and peculiar ways. The idea is not to minimize or deny gender a place in social research but to examine the role it plays as a topic itself deserving of sustained research attention. And, as Carol Warren and Jennifer Hackney make clear, there is much for us to learn.

John Van Maanen
Peter K. Manning
Marc L. Miller

PREFACE

The purpose of this second edition of *Gender Issues in Ethnography* is, like the first, to summarize the "state of the art" of gendered ethnography.[1] Our focus is more empirical than theoretical; using the literature on gender and ethnography, together with our own experiences as women ethnographers, we focus on the ways in which gender is experienced in the field. We seek to understand the ways the researcher experiences her or his own gender as well as the gender of respondents and the ways in which researchers represent these experiences through narrative. Both the doing and the writing of fieldwork are intertwined with gender (as well as with other cultural and bodily markers—"personal characteristics" such as age, class, ethnicity, or sexual identity).

In the decade or so since the last edition of *Gender Issues*, the inter-penetration of gender and other personal characteristics with the doing and writing of ethnography has moved beyond contestation. Indeed, the representation of the *respondent's* gender and other cultural markers has been supplanted, in some ethnographic quarters, by a focus on the *researcher's*. In place of the univocal ethnographer depicting intersubjective patterns among respondents, we find the polyvocality of individual respondents, each contributing their own narrative of self and gender (see, e.g., the essays in Lamphere, Ragone, & Zavella, 1997).

Even a decade ago, social scientists were concerned with the reflexive nature of fieldwork methods. The myth of the ethnographer as any person, without gender, personality, or historical location, who could objectively (at the very least intersubjectively) produce the same findings as any other person has been dispelled. Many of the early epistemological and methodological challenges to objectivity came from women researchers, who experienced the field differently from the androcentric fieldwork representations within which they had been trained. This resulted in a feminocentric cast to the ethnographic methods literature—looking at gender in the field meant looking at women in the field. This feminocentric cast is evident in the first edition of the book.

Over the past decade, the voices of men have been joined to those of women in the analysis of gender, with men's studies proliferating alongside women's. However, even a cursory perusal of the methodological fieldwork narrative indicates that writing about gendered ethnography remains primarily the provenance of women, perhaps because of the feminization of ethnography (and of some of the disciplines that practice it), perhaps because of the continuingly problematic nature of femaleness within social and academic life in a patriarchal society.

Some recent social science analysis is focused not on women or men but on gender as a subset of a broader field of power relations in contemporary postcapitalism. In this line of thought, the emphasis is on gender as a social structure rather than a characteristic of individuals or interactions. Campbell (1998), in reference to institutional settings, notes the shifting epistemological politics of ethnography in relation to gender and power:

> Dorothy E. Smith, long ago, called her work "sociology for women"; more recently, she and other researchers . . . have claimed that this form of analysis offers something for all those whose lives are subject to ruling relations. (p. 56)

Just as challenges to the idea of objectivity have become conventional wisdom in recent years, so have challenges to the idea of gender as an ascribed role rather than as a negotiated, situated feature of interaction. In the 1980s, Jennifer Hunt (1984) noted that the "older" studies of gender treated it as a fixed and essential characteristic of persons; although many ethnographers continue to treat gender as such, depictions of gender as negotiated and identity as situated have also become common as the 20th century moves into the 21st. Our view of gender as essential or as negotiated is that it is both: Respondents may see and treat gender as essential or negotiated, as may ethnographers. The more the narrative is fluid and unfixed (that, say, of the biracial or the bisexual), the more likely it seems to be that respondent and ethnographer join in the celebration of the fluid and the negotiable. Other ethnographies depict certainties of gender among populations such as children (Thorne, 1983) and working-class males (Yount, 1991)—although the ethnographer may not share such certainties.[2]

Feminist scholarship and epistemology have gained considerable influence in the humanities and social sciences today. Much of the contemporary work in gendered ethnography is also feminist, which has implications for the way in which ethnography is written—perhaps more for writing than for the conduct of the research itself (Arendell, 1997). Our approach to the study of gender is feminist, although it is not particularly postmodernist or experimental. The "warnings and advice" at the end of this volume refer more to "realist tales" (Van Maanen, 1988, p. 46), to the process and analytic of classic ethnography, than they do, say, to poems, plays, or performances.

Plan of the Book

The plan of the book is roughly similar to the first edition: gender in social science and social life; entrée, access, and relationships in fieldwork and interview; an analysis of gender methods narratives as representations; and, in the classical mode, "warnings and advice." Within these sections, there are changes in literatures and emphases, including more attention to interviewing, to the body, and to postmodernism.

In light of the expansion of the interview as a method of enhancing (or sometimes replacing) observation, we have added a discussion of gender and interviewing to this edition. Interestingly, although there is an enormous body of work from many fields on gender issues in field research, the literature on gender and ethnographic or intensive interviewing is still fairly sparse—indeed, the examination of interviewing as a qualitative method (as opposed to a tool for survey research) is still fairly sparse (Holstein & Gubrium, 1995). Although we take an interdisciplinary stance throughout the volume, drawing on sources from sociology, anthropology, communication studies, and education, we had to cast an even wider net for our interviewing than for our fieldwork material.

The body as an aspect of gender has become an important focus of scholarship during the last work, building on the work of Michel Foucault (1978, 1980) on the body, social control, and social order. In the first edition of *Gender Issues,* the material for the section on the body came mainly from anthropology, in which body differences between respondents and ethnographers (body shape, skin, hair, genitalia) were of significance to both. Now, both the body and the sexual (sex acts, sexual threats, sexual identity) are the object of analysis in sociology, cultural studies, and the other fields wherein ethnography is practiced.

The rise of postmodernism has clearly had an impact on the place of gender in social science and social life; it is no longer possible to frame ethnographic research in the ways described in the first edition, as the research of "any person." Despite the narrative turn in the humanities and social sciences—and the joining, in many narratives, of these two endeavors—we decided to keep the section on fieldwork as doing while expanding the discussion of fieldwork representation.[3] This is because we still, as ethnographers, *do*—we still interact with respondents (unless we confine ourselves to auto-ethnography), we still trust or mistrust respondents (and they us), and we still feel, think, get tired, gain or lose entrée, keep, or escape from our parts of the research bargain.

Which is why we still end with warnings and advice. We are both experienced field-workers, we are scholars, we are women; we have all kinds of scholarly as well as personal concerns—from children, to partners, to households—and all this affects our doing as well as our writing of ethnography. Those who do ethnography in the future are, we think, likely to be equally creatures of interaction as well as representation. Although representation is the end point of ethnography within the sphere of public scholarly discourse, it is not—yet, at any rate—all there is to fieldwork or to gender in the field.

Acknowledgments

Grateful thanks to our series editor, John Van Maanen, for liking the idea of a second edition, and to Don Stull for helping enormously with the anthropological parts. Special thanks to our Sage production staff, whose task was, this time, above and beyond.

GENDER ISSUES IN ETHNOGRAPHY

CAROL A. B. WARREN
JENNIFER KAY HACKNEY
University of Kansas

1. GENDER IN SOCIAL LIFE AND SOCIAL SCIENCE

In both Western and non-Western culture, being a woman or man is at the core of our social lives and our inner selves—unlike age, unchanging for most of us. There are exceptions and differences, but these exceptions and differences tend to highlight rather than suppress the essentialism of gender. For example, although transgendered people speak from the spaces between gender, transsexuals often seize on the essentialism of pure, dualistic gender to describe themselves, whereas transvestites perform the appearances that cultures use to express gender dualism to audiences (Gagne, Tewksbury, & McGaughey, 1997).

Gender is built into the social structure of Western and non-Western social orders, across time and space, permeating other hierarchies of race or status. Living within a society or visiting one as a field-worker presupposes gendered performances, interactions, conversations, and interpretations on the part of both researcher and respondents. Just as language reflects and establishes power relationships, all knowledge is gendered. The power-knowledge nexus genders cultural as well as structural space.

1

This intersection of knowledge, power, and gender in social life is currently at the core of feminist scholarship in the social sciences and humanities, a scholarship that is often interdisciplinary. And although there are feminist male ethnographers, most ethnographic writers on gender are women. This was not always so; early-20th-century ethnographic work was neither feminist nor gendered, and its canonical practitioners (with some notable exceptions, particularly Margaret Mead and Ruth Benedict) were male.

Contemporary scholarship on ethnographic practice during the 1920s to 1990s indicates the marginal status of women in the field, both the disciplinary field in which they practiced and the field into which they went to learn their craft. In sociology, ethnography began (as the case study) in Chicago. Although there were many women among the Chicago school sociology students of the 1920s to 1930s, the men Ph.D.s obtained tenure-track jobs in academia.[4] And it was not until the 1990s that the women of the Chicago school and their work became the focus of scholarly attention (Deegan, 1995; Lopata, 1995). Although attention was focused on women scholars somewhat earlier in anthropology, it is only recently that many of the once-marginal women who fed the stream of knowledge have been recognized for their contributions[5] (Parezo, 1993b).

Among the women sociologists currently engaged in the practice of social research are a number trained at the "second Chicago school"—the University of Chicago between 1945 and 1960. These women, who represented roughly 15% of the total of graduate students during this period, began their careers in secondary rather than tenure-track positions. As Deegan (1995) notes, "A number of our most eminent, contemporary women in sociology were . . . trained or employed in marginal positions in this era" (pp. 322-323). Still other women's names have been forgotten by the discipline; their names and dissertation titles read poignantly as follows:

Lilienthal, Daisy (Mrs. Taglizcozzo) "The Meaning of Unionism: a Study of the Perspectives of Members of the Plumbers' Union, the United Mine Workers, and the United Automobile Workers of America" 1956. . . . Carter, Wilmoth Annette, "The Negro Main Street of a Contemporary Urban Community" 1959. (Deegan, 1995, p. 328)

No woman held a tenured or tenure-track position at the University of Chicago in the era during which these women were trained (Deegan, 1995, p. 328).

Since those early days, women sociologists have appeared from coast to coast and in between as tenured professors and even department chairs. These women were trained by the second Chicago school, by the "California school," and by other schools that followed. The California school was shaped by Chicago and by the political ferments of the late 1960s and early 1970s, by labeling theory and "appreciation" of deviant worlds, and by the civil rights and women's movement. Since the 1960s—in all the fields of ethnography as well as sociology—gender has been incorporated not only into the ranks of academia but also into the theories, topics, and methods of our ethnographic trade.

Although it is now generally taken for granted, gender shapes the interactions in our settings; it shapes entrée, trust, research roles, and relationships—the entire epistemological field through which we, as fieldworkers, identify our methodological experiences. This "realist" set of concerns is the topic of the next section; despite the representational turn in ethnography, many—perhaps most—accounts of fieldwork presume actors, events, thoughts, and feelings behind the author's representations of them.

2. GENDER AND FIELDWORK RELATIONSHIPS

There is a vast literature on gender in fieldwork relationships—more so than other personal characteristics, such as ethnicity and age (perhaps because there are relatively more young women field-workers than either minority or elderly ones). This literature can be read—and in this section we so write it—as a reflection of interactions that occurred between gendered field-workers and respondents in time and space. The literature can also be read—and in following sections, we so write it—as a set of fieldwork representations, shaped by disciplinary rhetoric and conventions.

Themes in the literature on gendered fieldwork are built on earlier themes in the literature on fieldwork in general: the idea of ethnography as a series of reflexive and overlapping stages of entrée, process, and analysis. These themes have historically included entrée into the setting, finding a place, fieldwork roles and relationships, research bargains, trust and rapport, and leaving the field.[6] Gender both frames these stages and poses specific concerns, among the most salient of which are the place of the body, sexuality, and sexual identity among and between researchers and respondents.

4

In the 1980s, we saw a few confessional tales of sexual interest and attraction (Turnbull, 1986); at the turn of the millennium, a darker side of sexuality appears in ethnography. Themes of bodily and sexual danger inform turn-of-the-century narratives of gendered ethnography, the bodily danger of violence a concern of both females and males, but the specifically sexual dangers of assault or harassment more salient to women in the field.

In accounts of fieldwork from the 19th into the late 20th century, the presumption has been the encounter of the researcher as self with strangers and/or strange cultures as other (and the reflexivity of self and other that becomes possible within the process of coming-to-know). But in recent decades, there has been (we think) an increase in ethnographic research that starts precisely "where we are": researching one's own settings and identities. This movement toward or even into the realms of auto-ethnography has given a different turn to the stagelike depictions of entrée through leaving the field. As Adler and Adler (1987) note, writing about fieldwork methodology requires an understanding of the continuum of membership roles from stranger to complete member; gender in the field represents one aspect of this continuum.

Entrée and the Web of Gender

Entrée into the field ranges, depending on prior proximity to it, from events and meanings long ago accomplished to elaborate journeys into distant lands. In the first instance, entrée is represented by the decision to study the group of which one is a member and the further, consequent decisions about explaining the movement from member into member-researcher roles. Some researchers who begin to study their own settings (especially if and when they wish to do interviewing) relate their intentions to at least some fellow members (Krieger, 1986); others attempt, self-consciously, to keep their new scholarly motivations a secret, at least for the moment (Warren, in press).

Researchers may also locate their research beginnings "where they are" in focal concerns, which then prompt entrée into settings where these concerns are mediated. Issues of slenderness and body weight, for example, have prompted women researchers to explore the worlds and meanings of weight loss institutions, clinics, and self-help groups (Vogler, 1993; see also Warren, in press). In another variant of research entrée into the routinely familiar, ethnographers who volunteer or work in particular settings turn their attention to sociological and work-related tasks within the setting, effecting entrée as a researcher taking on other roles.

For the stranger confronting the other, the field-worker's initial reception by the host society reflects a cultural contextualization of the field-worker's characteristics, including marital status, age, physical appearance, presence and number of children, social class, and ethnic, racial, or national differences as well as gender.[7] In our own society, *sex* is generally considered a biological status, whereas *gender* refers to the ways in which biological sex roles are culturally elaborated: the values, beliefs, technologies, and general fates to which we assign women and men. Other cultures do not necessarily separate cultural from biological roles in this way; the view of biology as destiny is far more ancient and pervasive than our own ideology would permit. Nor do other cultures necessarily make the distinctions we do between sexual identity, gender identity, and sexual behavior; categories such as gayness, lesbianism, transsexualism, and transvestism are historically and culturally determined.

Yet sex and gender remain dominant organizing categories in most societies. And although gender intersects with other characteristics, women field-workers from the 1920s to the present have found their research—willingly or unwillingly—focused on women's issues and women's settings, mainly in the domestic sphere: child rearing, health, and nutrition. In part, this results from expectations associated with their home territory—with Western anthropologists' cultural assumptions. But in addition, the societies studied by anthropologists are often highly gender segregated, with gendered boundaries around public and domestic activities. Niara Sudarkasa (1986), for example, notes that in her study of the Yoruba,

> I was never expected to enter into, and never did see, certain aspects of the life of men in the town. I never witnessed any ceremonies that were barred to women. Whenever I visited compounds I sat with the women while the men gathered in the parlors or in front of the compounds.... I never entered any of the places where men sat around to drink beer or palm wine and to chat. (p. 181)

The gendering of fieldwork is a reflection of both the differential experiences of men and women in the field and (perhaps) their ways of reflecting on experience. When it has been possible to make comparisons, as in husband-wife anthropological teams, there are indications that the different ways in which females and males are defined and treated are reflected in different field notes. Ann Fischer (1986) says of her and her husband's fieldwork on the island of Truk in Micronesia that

> there was a marked contrast between the treatment of myself and my husband. When he visited me, my chair (the only one on the island) would be preempted for his use, and an informant would squat by his side, spending hours answering his questions. Formal arrangements would quickly be made to demonstrate for him some aspect of Trukese life in which he had expressed an interest. As a result, if our field notes are compared, my husband's record is of the more formal aspects of culture in exactitude, while mine tend to be a running account of what was happening in the village or in the homes in which I observed. The difference held in most of the cultures in which we did fieldwork together [including New England] . . . our access to data was different in every culture we studied, and although our interests and personalities may have contributed to some of these differences, our sex roles were also a most important element. (p. 282)

Women may have access to other women in the field by virtue of gender, marital status, or childbirth—and men to males—but spatial access does not mean access to the *meaning* of the worlds of informants. Sexuality and reproduction, for example, may be taboo topics among some women as well as between women and men. Nancie Gonzalez (1986) notes that married Guatemalan women with children consider it rude and embarrassing to discuss pregnancy or childbirth with both unmarried and with childfree women. Although a youthful Dona Davis (1986, p. 256) was able to converse freely with the middle-aged women of Newfoundland about sexuality and childbirth, when she asked specific interview questions about menopause, she shocked and alienated her respondents. A shared male status also can fail to guarantee access to the inner worlds of other men. Ernestine Friedl (1986) comments that in the Greek village she studied, the male role included a macho willingness to boast about sex, use sexual swear words, and make sexual jokes. But because her husband was a professor and thus of a higher class, the Greek village men would not do these things in his presence, just as they would not in her presence because of her gender. Friedl indicates that the couple obtained less information than they would have liked about the attitudes, values, and general behavior of young married men; despite the assistance of a male collaborator, she did not have one who was also young and of the same social class as the villagers. Abramson (1993), on the other hand, in his ethnography of the eastern interior of Fiji, became a chief among male chiefs, the focus of attention, "a great, mighty and fecund chief from Great Britain" (p. 67).

Margaret Mead (1986) has proposed that the conduct of women anthropologists in the field was, in earlier decades, influenced by the degree of her adoption of the traditional female role within her own culture (while she herself worked in a way that was not confined by her own generalizations). She argued that there were two styles of woman anthropologist: (a) the ones with deeply feminine interests and abilities who interest themselves, in the field, with the affairs of women and children and (b) the masculinely oriented ones, bored with women and children who wanted to work alone and attempt to use male informants and study male worlds (Mead, 1986). Contemporary anthropologists may also seek to identify with and study women in the field but from the standpoint of feminism rather than of the traditional female role within their own or another's culture (see, e.g., Bell, 1993).

Although women social scientists have historically sought access to male worlds, male social scientists have rarely, until recently, been interested in the sphere of women—which is in most cultures of the world of the domestic (and therefore by modern Western definitions insignificant)—except occasionally for comparative purposes (Fleuhr-Lobban & Lobban, 1986, p. 183). One exception is Black anthropologist Norris Brock Johnson's (1986, p. 167) fieldwork in a Midwestern U.S. elementary school. He attributed the initial resistance of the female teachers to his presence to the male hegemony in which female authority and territory were routinely undermined and female sexual status took precedence over professional status:

> Male custodians had free access and routinely sauntered into the classroom unannounced, mostly while classes were in session. Many times the [male] principal would walk into the classroom, without knocking, to make an announcement, often blithely interrupting the teacher. . . . The role and status of the female classroom teacher involved a gender expectation of subservience. . . . The gender expectation seemed to be that males are sexually aggressive toward females irrespective of place or situation. . . . [The teachers] wanted to find out if I was safe: that is would I recognize their professional status and act appropriately, or would I act like a man and exhibit sexually inappropriate behavior. (Johnson, 1986, pp. 167-168)

Johnson gained acceptance from the teachers over time by not acting like (his image of their image of) a traditional male: by respecting their authority and territory and by not flirting with them.

It is not only in non-Western societies that activities and places are seg-regated by gender. Sociologists and anthropologists who, like Johnson (1986), study Western locales, also encounter closed worlds and secret societies wholly or partially delimited by gender. For example, when Warren (1972) did her dissertation study of a male secretive gay com-munity during the late 1960s and early 1970s, she was able to do fieldwork in those parts of the setting dedicated to sociability and leisure—bars, par-ties, and family gatherings. She was not, however, able to observe in those parts of the setting dedicated to sexuality—even quasi-public settings such as homosexual bath houses (see Styles, 1979) and tearooms (see Humphreys, 1979). Thus, her portrait of the gay community was only a partial one, bounded by the social roles assigned to females within the male homosexual world.

Although diversity in gender norms may be witnessed between cul-tures, gender generally remains a central, organizing category. Yet it is not the only organizing category; it intersects with other characteristics that may or may not constitute central categories in our own culture. Two social institutions that, like gender, tend to have more pervasive cultural warrant are marriage and family. The field-worker's marital status is of particular significance to anthropological informants because most "primitive" cultures take kinship bonds as the fundamental source of social structure and social order. As Angrosino (1986) comments, "A sin-gle person is a rarity in most societies where anthropologists have done fieldwork" (p. 68). Furthermore, these dominant categories of gender, marital status, and parental status intersect. Although male anthropolo-gists seem to report fewer practical research problems with their unmar-ried status than women, they indicate that there is a nearly universal expectation that adult males should be sexually active (Angrosino, 1986; Back, 1993; Whitehead, 1986). An unmarried, childless adult woman has no fully legitimate social place in many non-Western cultures unless, per-haps, she is elderly and thus androgynized (Golde, 1970/1986). As Peggy Golde (1970/1986) said of her entrée into the culture of the Nahua Indians of Mexico,

What was problematic was that I was unmarried and older than was reason-able for an unmarried girl to be. I was without the protection of my family, and I traveled alone, as an unmarried, virginal girl would never do. They found it hard to understand how I, so obviously attractive in their eyes, could still be single. . . . Being an unmarried girl meant that I should not drink, smoke, go about alone at night, visit during the day without a real errand, speak of such topics as sex or pregnancy, entertain boys or men in my house except in the presence of older people, or ask too many questions of any kind. (p. 80)

Married women anthropologists fit some cultural expectations while violating others, often those concerned with gender dominance. Ernestine Friedl (1986), describing her fieldwork in a Greek village accompanied by her husband, commented,

> At the outset . . . I was involved in a formally and publicly wife-dominated enterprise in a society that was husband-centered to a degree even greater than is customary in Western Europe and America. Half deliberately and half as a matter of natural development we pragmatically compensated for this anomaly. My husband became the spokesman for the two of us in Athens and the village. (p. 198)

When the working partner in a marital team is a woman anthropologist and her husband is not working, he may be able to assume the main burden of household chores; indeed, an equalization of household labor seemed to become increasingly common among academics between the 1960s and 1980s (cf. Freedman, 1986; Oboler, 1986). But this etic adaptation can conflict with local cultural norms concerning the proper sphere of women's and men's work. During her fieldwork in Rumania, Diane Freedman (1986) noted that

> while the villagers knew that our own household customs differed from theirs, we were expected to conform somewhat to ideal patterns of the sexual division of labor. In this pattern, household and garden tasks are the domain of the women, and heavy agricultural work and the care of large animals are left to the men. . . . Our household was different since Robert had neither land to till nor animals to tend. As a result, he did more than half of our housekeeping. Villagers were scandalized by our customs on this issue. . . . Men's reaction[s] to our system [of drawing water from the well, done in the village by women, but in the Freedman household by Robert] were divided. Some thought it amusing, while others felt that Robert was degrading himself by doing women's work. The women, by contrast, considered it a positive sign of Robert's concern for me. Even the women, however, had limits of custom beyond which they would not be drawn. When they realized that Robert was also washing clothes, I was advised that he should do this in the house and that I should then hang the clothes outside; otherwise my reputation as a good wife would suffer. (pp. 344-345)

Not only marital status but also parenthood is a part of the field of characteristics by which host peoples often interpret the anthropological couple. Carolyn Fleuhr-Lobban says of her fieldwork in the Sudan that

> in a society where the extended family is the norm and the value placed on family life is high, there is no question in my mind that being identified as part of a family, originally with my husband and later with our daughter Josina, was an asset, possibly even a vital element in conducting successful field research. (Fleuhr-Lobban & Lobban, 1986, p. 188)

Motherhood is a potentially powerful source of mutual identification between anthropologist and respondent in the field. Macintyre (1993) notes that one respondent and friend, Edi, "seized on all similarities and denied the differences" between them, whereas male respondents generally did the opposite. In a conversation about contraception, birth, and illness in young children, Edi said that

> birth is the same for all women . . . we don't use these words. But I understand what you say, I understand you. Babies are all born in the same way. What you felt, I felt. But for you, only two, for me nine times. Oh my sister! (Macintyre, 1993, p. 48)

Regina Oboler (1986) reports a qualitative difference in her fieldwork after she became pregnant. Although pregnancy drained her physically, making the tasks of fieldwork more difficult, it had a positive effect on field relationships. She said that as news of her pregnancy spread among her Kenyan informants,

> a remarkable thing happened: my rapport with the women, which I already thought was quite good, took a sudden, dramatic turn for the better. In people's minds I had moved from the category "probably barren woman" to "childbearing woman," similar to a change of gender. . . . Men who had been urging Leon [her husband] to take a second wife no longer did so. (p. 45)

But it is not always feasible or desirable for anthropologists to bring their children into the field. When children are left behind, mothers' (and perhaps fathers') experiences of the field are colored by the feelings of absence. Macintyre (1993), encountering a child on a pathway on her second day on Tubetube Island in Papua New Guinea, commented,

I looked at my watch and wondered if my daughters were dressed and ready to go to school in Fremantle. It was a long time before a day went past and I didn't worry about their punctuality and whether or not they would be collected from school at the right time. (pp. 45-46)

Gender and its intersections with other field-worker characteristics can provide and limit access to various settings and topics. Gender also frequently serves to define appropriate and inappropriate behaviors. Within this web of appropriate and inappropriate, accessible and inaccessible, we may also locate ourselves along a continuum of invisible and hypervisible. Mixed-gender organizations in which men are generally in dominant and women in subordinate positions can be ideal for women researchers. Research in such organizations has taught us about the invisibility of the servant female in Western society. Even as we begin the 21st century, women in organizations, although they may sometimes be CEOs, still are generally the secretaries and clerks. Wandering around settings such as a psychiatric hospital and a court and even investigating the contents of file drawers drew Warren (1982) hardly a glance from the males engaged in "more important business." Other women field-workers report similar experiences of invisibility. After all, the social place of women in Western society has traditionally been to stand behind men, out of their sight: as mothers, wives, nurses, secretaries, and servants.

FINDING A PLACE

The field-worker who is not part of her own setting may enter the setting with a social place in mind: to do volunteer work, perhaps, or hang out on the street corner and become part of the passing scene; to help out with building houses; or teach nursery school. But this process of finding a place is reciprocal: The respondents also have a voice in where they place the field-worker and, indeed, may have the ability to refuse to place her at all—to send her packing. If allowed to stay, the field-worker may find herself the subject of many interpretations and given a variety of social places within which she may feel comforted or of little comfort.

The man or woman entering a strange culture is a stranger; most non-Western cultures are today familiar with strangers. Foreign men and women who appear and make themselves at home in a Sudanese village, a Rumanian school, or a Newfoundland town are part of the landscape of contemporary life. Their place in the society—according to Hunt (1984), their gender—is negotiated from the existing cultural stock of knowledge

and action available to define and cope with strangers. The didactic methodological literature (e.g., Bailey, 1996; Lofland & Lofland, 1984) focuses on the problem of researcher-as-stranger role stance: what role to adopt in a given setting, whether overt or secret, seeker or savant.

Our own research experience (most recently in various self-help, medical, psychiatric, and legal organizations) has led us to conclude that role taking in fieldwork is subsumed by a more interactive process in which respondents assign the field-worker to what they see as her or his proper place in the social order. When Hackney (1996a, 1996b) did participant observation in an eating disorders support group, for example, she was defined by others present as a member with an eating disorder, despite her stated interest in attending the group for research purposes and her refusal to label herself as someone in need of psychological help. In both the mental health court and mental hospitals Warren (1982) studied, where young women were typically either law students or assistants or visiting nursing students, she was treated as one or another of these social types, even by people to whom she had mentioned, more than once, that she was a professor and a researcher. Male visitors, on the other hand, were more often taken for attorneys, psychiatrists, or (again) law students, never nursing students or nurses. During Warren's (1972) research in the secret gay community in the late 1960s, she was often defined as a "fag hag" (in other locales, a "faggotina" or "fruit fly"), a fairly harmless if buffoonish role. The male gay community at this time assigned roles to heterosexual (and, to a lesser extent, lesbian) women based on their participation in the sociable (certainly not the sexual) dimensions of the subculture. The fag hag was a woman perceived as afraid of or alienated from the world of straight men, who had found unthreatening fun and attention in the gay world (Warren, 1972).

KEEPING A PLACE

When researchers are already members of the settings they choose to study, entrée is unproblematic—they are already there. What may become problematic is not entrée and finding a place but rather "keeping" their place or negotiating a new one. Many field-workers and interviewers who have chosen to make their life worlds into ethnographic settings have found that they experience dislocations from these worlds in the ethnographic or interviewing act; they lose their place, or their place changes. Back (1993), for example, in his study of a South London adolescent community, began "where he was": "My choice of doctoral research was closely related to my own experience. I was born in South London in the early 1960s, of white working-class parents" (p. 221). He adds, "To my present embarrassment, I used my working-class origins as a way of gaining credit for this research and thus fictitiously dissolving the division between self and other" (p. 222).

What Back no longer was, however, was an adolescent or a participant in the racist commentaries of the White adolescent subculture. Self was no longer other or other self. Studying masculinities as a scholar who had joined a world of feminism and antiracism, his research was not only a journey into the field but a way of understanding the relationship between self, setting, and the passage of time: "Making our 'selves' seen is about making our masculinities the subject of discussion" (Back, 1993, p. 230).

Ifi Amadiume (1993), an Eastern Nigerian anthropologist trained at the University of London, returned to her extended family in Nnobi to do fieldwork, where her gendered, statused "rightful kinship place in the society" immersed her in "accepted and expected patterns of reciprocity" (p. 196). Amadiume claims that persistent accusations against anthropologists of being Eurocentric, racist, or spies are grounded in the lack of place that a stranger, as well as her or his project, has within this local culture of kin reciprocity. "If a stranger or anthropologist is not herself or himself a social subject or part of the field of study, what could possibly justify the study of another society?" (Amadiume, 1993, p. 196). Although Amadiume's analysis challenges the place of the (non-Western) stranger in field research, Back's (1993) analysis challenges the place of the nonstranger.

For researchers studying groups in which they already have membership, the issue of "keeping" one's place may be particularly salient. However, for both members and strangers, research relationships and roles are never static but are characterized by continual shifts and displacements as fieldwork interactions progress.

Research Relationships and Roles

Whether one is female or male, stranger or familiar, it is inevitable that during the course of fieldwork, relationships are formed. These relationships may be marked by easy rapport and egalitarian stances, by dominance and submission, and by tension and conflict—changing, perhaps, from one moment to the next. If any length of time is spent in the field, then it is more than likely that the nature of relationships and roles the fieldworkers find themselves in will change. Again, the didactic methodological literature tends to focus on the perspective of the researcher, implicitly or explicitly arguing that the researcher *takes* a stance or a role: The researcher chooses a place along the continuum of distance or immersion, a stance of observer or participant, a role of alien or native (Adler & Adler, 1987).

In addition to emphasizing the power of the field-worker, the literature also tends to portray relationships as static; once the researcher has obtained a place, that place is more or less maintained throughout the research process. In contrast, we view the roles and relationships of the field-worker as the dynamic and fluid processes of interaction and negotiation. Although the field-worker may seek to find or keep a particular place, respondents are simultaneously putting her into a place. Furthermore, the place the researcher seeks or finds herself or himself in changes situationally and over time.

FICTIVE KIN

Depending on the culture and the field-worker (her or his gender, social ties, and projects), the roles into which the stranger is tentatively fitted can range from spy to adoptive child or both as they change over time. Anthropologists, especially young married women, are often assigned roles of "fictive kin": adoptive daughter or child, brother, sister, or mother (Golde, 1970/1986). Jean Briggs (1986) describes the role of Kapluna daughter she was given among the Eskimo:

> Categorization of me as a child was probably determined by several factors: I had introduced myself as one who wanted to learn . . . and I had asked to be adopted as a daughter; I was obviously ignorant of [the culture's] proprieties and skills. The fact that I am a woman may also have facilitated my categorization as a child in several respects. . . . In order to be considered properly adult a woman must have children, and I had none . . . the role of an adult woman was virtually closed to me, whereas had I been a man I might have earned an adult role as a fisherman and hunter, as some [males] who have lived among Eskimos appear to have done. (p. 40)

The child role, with a married couple as "field father and mother," also characterized Karim's (1993) depiction of her research relationships among Carey Islanders. She notes that "my single female status positioned me in the role of a daughter to Mijah my field mother. Initially a short term arrangement, everyone found this to be acceptable, and I finally began to relax and enjoy the fieldwork experience" (Karim, 1993, p. 83).

Other "family" roles may be extended to women or men anthropologists. Laura Nader (1986) notes that in her study of the Shias in Lebanon, she was placed in the role of "sister to men . . . a natural role that a woman anthropologist could walk into, should she wish. I did exactly that" (p. 111).

Examples in the literature of males being assigned a kinship role are encountered more rarely. This may be the result of hosts being less likely to bestow this kind of status on researchers or the result of male researchers being less likely to view a relationship in this way. Still, examples do exist; in his research on the Caribbean island of Bequia, in the Grenadines, Johnson (1986) explores the ways in which the Bequia male role in general and the role of shipbuilder in particular echoed his own gender socialization. Not only was he fitted into place by his informants, but he felt the fit, he wanted the fit, and the fit involved his sense of self and his own biography. He describes his relationship with a key informant, a master shipbuilder:

> Men use tools to manipulate the elements and bring them under control, something I think men universally tend to admire in each other. Quite consciously, then, I sought to exhibit my [competence with tools]. . . . I remember feeling quite like a child trying to get my father's attention. I was a male coming to understand and trying to acquire his approval. (Johnson, 1986, pp. 173-174)

THE HONORARY MALE

Women's invisibility in Western cross-gender settings and immurement in women's worlds in the non-Western have prompted some women field-workers to devise ways of attempting access into men's worlds.[8] Older women anthropologists, writing in the 1980s, inscribed themselves as androgynized, something they saw as possible in cultures where older native women were allowed male privileges (Golde, 1970/1986). Both whiteness and foreignness, as well as aging, may permit women fieldworkers more cross-gender behavior than that allowed to native women, giving rise to the concept of the woman anthropologist as "honorary male." Carolyn Fleuhr-Lobban comments that in her fieldwork in the Sudan,

> As a woman with a husband and later a young daughter, I was not afforded the status of honorary male which many Western female professionals living alone in the Sudan receive. However, as a white female Westerner . . .

engaged in research and attached to a family, my status was more ambiguous
than Richard's, and as a result I had more social mobility in the system than
he did. For example I could, if I wanted, sit with men alone or with my husband present. (Fleuhr-Lobban & Lobban, 1986, p. 188)

Other anthropologists have found these quasi-male statuses to be either
temporary or perhaps illusory. Jean Jackson (1986) found that "after a
period of time, my femaleness had superseded my status as an affluent and
high-status outsider" (p. 271). She adds, "I was both elated and irritated.
. . . Although more of an insider, I was being assigned to my proper place
on the inside—second place" (p. 271). Similarly, Hutheesing (1993) notes
that among the Thai lowland people she studied, her "adjustment" to par-
ticipating in Lisu womanhood increasingly involved being placed into the
gender roles of that society, which "entail [my] being made to feel a lesser
being in comparison with the male" (p. 97).

Rather than fitting in some clear-cut way to local gender arrangements,
either the field-worker or the respondents may interpret gender more am-
biguously or situationally. Rena Lederman (1986), among the Mendi, was

concerned with not aligning myself clearly with either the men or the women
(as I understood the difference then). . . . I hoped to take advantage of whatever ambiguity my outsider status afforded, sidestepping the issue of my own
gender and commitments for a while, if possible. (p. 378)

Although geographical foreignness plays a part in negotiated roles, it is
not the only type of outsiderness that can be brought to an interaction.
Jennifer Hunt (1984) describes the various ways in which she attempted to
become accepted in the Western, gender-stratified world of urban police.
There she had

to convince police subjects that I was a trustworthy person who could conduct honest research. I had to negotiate a gender identity that combined ele-
ments of masculine trustworthiness with feminine honesty. I therefore
become a liminal person who dwelled between two opposing realms of the
policeman's symbolic world. (p. 286)

Hunt (1984) describes the urban police world as one dominated by a
hierarchy of authority and a polarization of gender. Power relations are
structured by the differentiation between elite (administrative) and street
police, and

gender is an essential aspect of identity . . . characterized by a structural and symbolic split between a feminine/domestic and a masculine/public domain. . . . Police distinguish between moral and non-moral persons, and between clean and dirty domains. These distinctions of morality and space are both mediated by gender. Thus superior moral virtue and honesty are perceived as feminine attributes of women who work in the clean world of the home. In contrast, corruption and dishonesty are viewed as masculine characteristics of men who work in the vice-ridden public sphere. In this case, the women of the home are viewed as untrustworthy in part because their superior feminine virtue is seen as dangerous in a public world in which most members are corrupt. In contrast, men who work on the street are perceived as trustworthy mainly because they share an involvement in illicit activity. (Hunt, 1984, p. 286)

Hunt (1984) proposes that her respondents interpreted her gender situationally. At times, she was the honorary male:

Pistol practice provided the perfect opportunity to display the esteemed characteristics of masculine aggression and heart. One day I was practicing combat shooting and, as usual, my score was abominable. Ashamed, I left the range with my target hidden so no one could see it. However, a pistol instructor and several unknown off-duty officers approached and asked how I did. I responded, "not so good today, but tomorrow I'll blow the mother's guts out." Astonished, one officer commented, "Did you hear what she said?!" They both smiled and nodded approvingly. I had shown that I was not a passive woman but a competent man who could feel just as violent as they. (Hunt, 1984, p. 290)

In other situations within the shifting moments of gender and authority in the police world, Hunt was a dyke, whore, spy, date, or traditional woman:

The feminine aspects of my gender identity were ritually restored in a [playful judo] game played with an academy instructor [in which Hunt allowed herself to be overpowered]. . . . In this ritual, the sexual order of power was restored: the tough judo player was transformed into a weak helpless woman. (Hunt, 1984, p. 293)

THE FIELD-WORKER AS SPY

Gendered conceptions of the field-worker as spy occur against a background of criticism (by informants, social sciences, or other audiences) of the method itself as a form of spying. Charlotte Allen's (1997) article

18

"Spies Like Us" is only the latest of a long series of methodological and ethical debates over fieldwork methods as spying and deception. She quotes Kai Erikson as complaining about ethnographers who study religious groups or Alcoholics Anonymous: "We don't know how much harm it does to research subjects" (Allen, 1997, pp. 36-37). Allen cites several examples of ethnographic work and publication subsequent to which groups of respondents felt that they had been betrayed by researchers, including the people portrayed by Carolyn Ellis in *Fisher Folk* (1986), which "transformed her in their eyes from a beloved outsider and frequent guest into a traitor" (Allen, 1997, p. 31).

Gender and globalization set the context for the attribution of spying to social scientists in non-Western settings. The presence of a stranger in a Burmese village or an urban police department may prompt host informants to share their lives with an honorary male or adopted child, but it can also provoke suspicions of spying. Both in the world of macropolitics—where CIA agents have become covert instruments of U.S. policies—and in the micropolitics of organizations—where an arm of local government may be seeking information—one place to which the field-worker may be assigned is that of spy. And gender is one of several features of the field-worker and of her or his task that elaborate the role of spy. Depending on the social and political context, a female stranger can be invisible (field-worker as file clerk) or hypervisible (field-worker as Mata Hari).

In the late 1930s in Brazil, Ruth Landes (1986, p. 126) provoked suspicion that she was a spy in part because she lacked the obligatory male protector. She, in turn, found her actions the subject of Brazilian spying. Although Hazel Hitson Weidman was welcomed in the Burmese village she studied as a daughter and benefactress, she later found that she had been seen as a spy for the Burmese or the U.S. government (Weidman, 1986, p. 255). American social scientists doing research in socialist countries such as Cuba and Rumania (Freedman, 1986) have also been suspected of spying either for the U.S. or the native government. Karim's field-father on Carey Island tells her of the possible identities the islanders discussed for her, which included that of spy:

> When you came here two years ago without any warning, the village said you were a government spy. They said you had come to gather information about the land to resettle us elsewhere. Some said you were a head hunter and had come here to collect a few heads to fortify a new bridge on the mainland. Yet others said you were merely assuming a human form and would transform in

the middle of the night into a tigress and eat us all. You . . . probably . . . could assume animal or human forms. (Karim, 1993, p. 78)

Using her knowledge about gender roles on the island, with their assumptions of women's lesser powers, Karim asked him, "Why did they mistrust me, a woman?" Her field-father replied,

What difference does it make whether you are a woman or a man? It's the intention and the motive that matters. Formerly animals tried to overrun us by assuming human forms; these humans were not [real]. But I took you in. I knew you did not have these powers. I knew you were properly human. I made you my daughter. (Karim, 1993, p. 78)

The relationship between gender and the suspicion of spying is a complex one. Because in most cultures, males are perceived as more political, more linked to the sources of power, and more dangerous than females, they may be more readily taken for spies (see Back, 1993). Yet the sexualization of spying is associated with women and with the potent cultural symbolism of Mata Hari—the snake woman luring the hapless male into betrayal and doom.

The literature on organizations indicates that a field-worker whose gender does not fit with prevailing assumptions may be taken for a spy. Johnson (1986), for example, reports that in his study of elementary school teachers, all of whom were female, he was initially seen as a spy for the administration. Jennifer Hunt (1984) notes that any stranger doing research on urban police is liable to definition as a spy, but a woman even more so. Not only was the police department she studied embroiled in a lawsuit charging gender discrimination against female officers, but also

the role of spy was consistent with my gender identity. As a civilian and a moral woman I respected the formal order of law and the inside world of the academy. As both FBI and police internal security also represented the formal order, it was logical to assume I was allied with them. In addition, no policeman believed a woman was politically capable of fighting the department to promote honest research: Instead, the dominant elite would use me for their own purposes. (Hunt, 1984, p. 289)

INCORPORATION

Whether seen as man, woman, sorcerer, or honorary male, the field-worker who enters into a setting and stays a day or a year is incorporated into that setting; a niche within the host culture is carved for the ethnographer as the locals interpret and explain her or his presence within their own cultural frameworks. The place or role that the field-worker is given may be that of stranger, outsider, or deviant, or it may be a location of fictive kin or insider or familiar. But most commonly, it seems that the field-worker is incorporated with a dual status of insider and outsider, a familiar deviant, a stranger within. Contemporary field-workers are concerned to understand the processes of incorporation in relation to gender. Rena Lederman (1986), for example, found that the Mendi people of New Guinea placed her in that "deviant" female category "reserved for ambitious, opinionated Mendi women with many . . . projects of their own apart from their husbands and with reputations for talking out loudly" (p. 384). Laura Nader's (1986, pp. 104-105) behavior, outside the frame of traditional female, so puzzled the Zapotec Indians that they decided that she was able to turn herself into a man or woman at will. The Micronesians studied by Ann Fischer (1986, p. 276) were afraid that if she wandered into areas where white faces were not a familiar sight, she might be mistaken for a ghost and attacked. Hutheesing (1993) notes that in her fieldwork in Thailand,

> As a middle-aged foreign woman, I gained an extra prestige dimension to my "face." Besides being meted out the usual respect and courtesy, I was also given the privilege of entering the village shrine of the most senior ancestor spirit, an otherwise forbidden domain for women. (p. 97)

Repudiating the honorary male role ("whatever that really means"), with its implicit claim of actual membership within the gender hierarchy of the host community, Macintyre (1993) explores her incorporation into Papua New Guinea society. From having "no rightful place" she became, over time, an "incorporated anomaly." As an older married woman with children, she was incorporated through women's discourse; by her ethnicity and heritage, she remained an anomaly. Similarly, Abramson (1993) refers to the process of "assimilation" or "stereotyping . . . accommodation" by which he was accepted as a "brother" of chiefs in Carey Island (p. 67). He was incorporated as a male of high and chiefly status, but his youthful and unmarried status contrasted with that of the other chiefs. Macintyre speculates that women may incorporate or be incorporated more readily than men:

> Although I was unaware of it at the time . . . women instructed me as if I were being incorporated, whereas men more often used the exclusive "we," espe-

cially as "we Tubetube people" or "we Bwanabwana" [small islands] people. (Macintyre, 1993, p. 49)

Embodiment

That all of our experiences are embodied ones is increasingly being recognized within social scientific fields of study. Fieldwork, like all other experiences, is an embodied one: We peer through our own flesh to see the other, and we present our own flesh to the other while we are engaged in the act of observation—and this embodiment has consequences for our research.

The web of gender denotes not only one's place in the social structure but also the deep structure of human experience: the embodied self, with its experiences of sexuality, emotion, and sensation. What is presented to the host culture is a body: a size and shape, hair and skin, clothing and movement, sexual invitation or untouchability. The embodied characteristics of the male or female field-worker affect not only the place in the social order to which he or she is assigned but also the field-worker's and informants' feelings about attractiveness and sexuality, bodily functions, and display. Some of the ways in which the self is presented—such as hairstyle and clothing—can be altered; some—such as skin color and hand size—cannot. Thus, the process of developing relationships in the field involves the monitoring and (perhaps) modification not only of behavior but also of the researcher's body and its uses in the field.

In recent years, the body has become the focus of an interdisciplinary scholarship, grounded in feminist theory and an appreciation of the work of Michel Foucault (1978, 1980), focused on the body as text of culture. This work on the body has become incorporated into the more postmodernist ethnographies, such as Lamphere, Ragone, and Zavella's (1997) chapter, "Part II: Reproducing the Body," in *Situated Lives: Gender and Culture in Everyday Life.* In line with the postmodernist turn toward the text, most of the six chapters in this section of *Situated Lives* are concerned with discourses of the body, and Western ones at that, rather than doing embodied fieldwork in non-Western settings. Behar (1995) notes the embodiment of women respondents and the disembodiment of women anthropologists in fieldwork representations:

In anthropology it is always the other woman, the native woman somewhere else, the woman who doesn't write . . . the Balinese woman, the *National Geographic* woman, who has breasts. Breasts that can be seen, exposed, pictured, brought home, and put into books. The woman anthropologist, the woman who writes culture, also has breasts, but she is given permission to conceal them behind her pencil and pad of paper. Yet it is at her own peril that she deludes herself into thinking her breasts do not matter, are invisible, cancer won't catch up with them, the male gaze does not take them into account. (pp. 1-2)

DRESS AND APPEARANCE

One way in which the field-worker signals status and place is through dress and bodily adornment. This feature of appearance is the most amenable to modification, and modification (or lack thereof) is often important in the negotiation of roles and relationships. In the late 1960s, Warren was employed with several other graduate students in research involving the use of police records. Cordial relations with police officers at the various locations where we had to examine records daily could be maintained only by strict conformity to conservative codes of dress and appearance for men and women. At that particular historical juncture, facial hair and long hair on males had come to symbolize political protest, student status, and youthful privilege, a combination enraging to those, such as police, who supported the Vietnam War, regarded students as effete draft dodgers, and resented what they saw as the simultaneous flouting and flaunting of upper-middle-class privilege. Thus, males hired for the project had to cut their hair and shave and wear jackets and ties rather than the frayed jeans and worn tennis shoes favored by graduate students at the time. Dress and adornment are changeable—and changes are often necessary, as generations of anthropologists have learned.

Sometimes the research task is facilitated by wearing clothes that are the same as one's hosts, sometimes not. Hazel Hitson Weidman (1986) describes her adoption of the typical Burmese woman's style: "I selected flowered [long robes] that appealed to their tastes, and I sat with propriety, as a modest, well-bred young woman should. I wore fragrant body lotion, lipstick, earrings . . . and flowers in my hair" (p. 256). Weidman's attire seems to have been well chosen. In contrast, during her fieldwork in Madras, India, Penny Vera-Sanso (1993) made an initial mistake:

I decided initially against wearing a sari. . . . Instead, I had a tailor make up three sets of matching long dirndl skirts and blouses. . . . To my bewilderment I was continually being told I would look much better in a sari but nobody would say why. It was only after a few weeks into the research, when I noticed a young schoolgirl wearing more or less the same clothes, that I realized I had dressed myself as a prepubescent girl! (p. 162)

Different dress and hairstyles may be adopted to fit into the culture's gender roles, to disassociate oneself from those roles for some particular purpose, or to satisfy other demands based on age or social class. In their fieldwork in a Greek village, both Ernestine Friedl and her husband found that they were expected to wear certain clothes and avoid others. Because he was a professor, Robert was expected to dress daily in a suit and tie. Ernestine was allowed to dress less formally,

> but the villagers drew the line at letting me wear a standard village woman's kerchief to guard against the sun, because that was clearly a symbol of the rural woman who works in the fields and I was allowed only partially to simulate the position of village women. (Friedl, 1986, pp. 213-214)

One aspect of appearance that is often a crucial issue among respondents and informants is skin color, and although the interpretation and valuation of skin tone may vary, this feature is one over which the fieldworker has little, if any, control. Skin tone (and other physical characteristics) can signal racial and ethnic background, and similarities and differences from respondents in this regard affect the processes of fieldwork. In a world where colonialism has left its mark on so many cultures, fair skin and Caucasian physical characteristics result in the field-worker being perceived not only as a foreigner but also as someone of a higher status than the respondents. Fair skin is both attractive and distancing in the double status and relational systems within which postcolonial peoples live. Angrosino (1986) defines skin color as part of the

> dual socialization [in] colonial societies. Members of such societies are typically taught to revere the behaviors and standards of the metropolitan power; this external value system is termed a system of respectability. . . . [But] they must still function in the local social networks: the systems of the indigenous values that orient a person's life [are] termed a system of reputation. . . . Actions, vocabulary, gestures, associations, styles of dress, of eating, of housing, types of personal relationships, and so forth are all clearly demarcated as to their respectable or reputable character, and the individual's social persona is evaluated in terms of which system's character predominates. (p. 65)

The value placed on light skin in many of the cultures studied by anthropologists is one reflection of the impact of Western cultural imperialism on the non-Western world. The white- or light-skinned person is the respectable one, the rich and powerful one, and therefore the one desired and desirable. White, foreign female anthropologists, although they lack the superior status of males, are placed within the host culture's intersecting hierarchies of gender, ethnicity, and class through their association with the dominant Western culture. Peggy Golde (1970/1986) found that her whiteness and appearance made her attractive to the Nahua:

> Fair skin was a highly prized attribute, and the girls who were considered most beautiful were all distinctly light-skinned. I also had curly hair, another much envied attribute, which symbolized white blood. And I was plump, a characteristic that further enhanced my desirability in their eyes. (p. 79)

Both Golde (1970/1986) and Weidman (1986) noted that their light skin and physical desirability partially offset the limits to research access imposed by being a stranger, a foreigner, and female.

Social scientists designated Black in our U.S. racial classification system have provided accounts of the varying significance of the intersection of ethnicity and gender in the field. There are cultures and situations in which a dark skin color is desirable; Niara Sudarkasa (1986, pp. 174-176) was assigned the Yoruba role of a child who has come home on the basis of her status as a Black American.[9] But even in non-White cultures, light skin may be seen as preferable to dark. In describing his fieldwork in Jamaica, Black anthropologist Tony Larry Whitehead (1986) described his designation by the people of Haversham (the village he studied) as a "big, brown, pretty-talking man." "Big," as he comments, referred not to his size but to his presumed high status as an educated foreigner, and "pretty-talking" signaled his use of standard rather than dialect English. "Brown" was the term used by local Jamaicans to refer to light skin color in combination with its association with possession of material wealth and high morals. His high status and "respectability" were not necessarily beneficial to the research process, however, as Whitehead notes, "My bigness and pretty talk caused numerous data collection difficulties at the beginning of my fieldwork. Lower-income males did not want to talk to me . . . they answered me with meaningless yes sirs, and no sirs" (p. 215).

Although skin tone may be the embodied characteristic least amenable to change and dress the most, other aspects of bodily appearance associated with adornment or ritual are salient to a variety of cultures, and modifications, although possible, may be deemed as undesirable by the field-worker. Scarring, nose and neck enlargement, foot binding, plastic surgery, clitoridectomies, and circumcision have all been used to symbol-ize membership in a people, adherence to gender norms, proper adorn-ment, or medical hygiene. The extensive literature on natives' body modifications by anthropologists contrasts with the lack of comment on researchers' own conformity or nonconformity with these body norms and its research consequences. One exception is Oboler's (1986) analysis of her husband's acceptance among the Nandi and its bodily contingencies:

> His first trip to the river to bathe was a crucial test. In a spirit of camara-derie, as same-sex communal bathing is customary, he was accompanied by a number of young men. Tagging along was an enormous group of curiosity-seeking children and younger adolescents . . . everyone wanted to know the answer: . . . Was Leon circumcised? In Nandi, male initiation involving ado-lescent circumcision is the most crucial event in the male life cycle, without which adult identity, entry into the age-set system, and marriage are impossi-ble. . . . Fortunately Leon, a Jew by ancestry and rearing, passed the test. I be-lieve that an uncircumcised husband would have made fieldwork in Nandi extremely difficult for me. (p. 37)

Although clitoridectomy or "female circumcision" (removal of the cli-toris and sometimes other portions of the labia) was formerly practiced among the Nandi, it was rare at the time of Oboler's (1986) fieldwork, par-ticularly among the educated. Carolyn Fleuhr-Lobban and Lobban (1986) note that clitoridectomy was practiced extensively in the northern Sudan at the time she and her husband did their field research, despite govern-mental attempts to limit the practice. But she gives no indication of how her nonconformity to this deeply held and felt body norm affected her acceptance among the adult women she studied.

The relationship between gender and the body was illuminated for Pat Caplan (1993b) when she wanted to have a film made of a circumcision rit-ual involving some of her male fictive kin on the Tanzanian island of Mafia. As a woman, she could not attend the ceremony. But she found that the village men would have preferred her attendance at the ceremony over the attendance of uncircumcised men. Although gender defined the out-sider, the body defined it even more clearly:

Villager: . . . we want to know if those men (the crew) have been circumcised?

[Pat]: I really do not know, but I will ask.

Villager: Because if they have not, then it would have been better for you to be there and have taken the pictures than strangers like them. (Caplan, 1993b, p. 173)

Studies of body modification seem to be proliferating in the 1990s. James Myers (1992) studied "Nonmainstream Body Modification: Genital Piercing, Branding, Burning and Cutting" among a San Francisco group. Still, sociological studies within this new genre of the body tend toward the abstract, conceptual, and disembodied. Myers's entrée into this body-exhibiting group was premised on the members' desire for the gaze of the other—in some ways, an ideal setting for the questing body-scholar: "The people I interviewed and observed were for the most part barely subdued exhibitionists who took joy in displaying and discussing their body and its alterations" (Myers, 1992, p. 271).

Myers's status as an outsider, a male college professor, proved to be no barrier to entrée or observation in this exhibitionistic space; the woman he contacted at a San Francisco organization promoting genital piercing said, "Good god yes! You're welcome to come. We need people to see that just because we're kinky doesn't mean we're crazy too" (Myers, 1992, p. 270).

SEX

Sex is a focal theme in all cultures in one way or another—what to do about and with bodies, sexual acts, intercourse, taboos, identities, and if, when, and how to talk about these things—and the culture of fieldwork publication is no different. The discourse of sexuality in the ethnographic field seems to have changed historically: from public silence (outside unpublished diaries and correspondence) or warnings of sexual danger to women in the field (the 1920s to 1950s); an examination of others' motivations, imputations, and unwanted overtures (the 1960s and 1970s); a discussion of mutual sexual attraction and activity between field-workers and informants (in the 1980s); and most recently a return to the issue of sexual danger (in the 1990s). This historical discourse on sexuality is itself a gendered one, with different female and male themes.

Although silence in published accounts was the rule of thumb in the first half of the 20th century, the question of (hetero) sexuality in fieldwork first publicly arose in the context of the safety from the rape of White women alone in the field. There was little consideration among academics in the 1920s or 1930s of the possibility of the mutual attraction of a White woman scholar and her non-White male informants. But even in this era, in cultures in which there was no legitimate role open to an unattached woman, locals might assign heterosexual motives to her. During her field-work in Brazil in the late 1930s, for example, Ruth Landes (1986, p. 137) was accused of seeking vigorous men to do more than carry her luggage. Indeed, Landes was labeled a prostitute during her research in the face of inadvertent violations of gender proprieties. On one occasion, she checked into a hotel that, unknown to her, was frequented by prostitutes, and on another occasion, she wore a type of shoe worn locally only by streetwalkers (pp. 130-132). Diane Freedman (1986) also found that her marital status affected informants' perceptions of her motivations. Re-turning to a Rumanian village as a widow and unattached woman, she found that in contrast to her earlier fieldwork as a married woman,

> my behavior was interpreted differently; friendly interactions were seen as indication of illicit behavior. My need for friendship and approval led me to participate in gatherings where cross-sex joking was common, and I was of-ten the focus of the jokes. I interpreted these events on a surface level, as jokes in a friendly spirit. But the underlying theme was more serious than I realized at the time. (Freedman, 1986, p. 357)

All societies have conceptions of what constitutes licit and illicit sex. Cross-culturally, the legitimation of sexual activity has most often been through marriage, an institution that links the sexual to the social, the pub-lic to the private, and one generation to the next. Ethnographers have encounters with what the culture deems licit, as well as illicit, sexuality. Indeed, the typical experience of the unmarried, young female anthropol-ogist—especially if she is made further desirable by foreignness, apparent wealth, light skin, and adoption of local dress and appearance norms—is to become the object of marriage proposals. In Peggy Golde's (1970/ 1986) research among the Nahua Indians, for example, she found herself subjected to attempts at persuasion to

> marry in the village. . . . In trying to persuade me, they would argue that I wasn't too old for the marriageable boys of fifteen, sixteen, or seventeen, since older women quite frequently married younger boys. This was a patent untruth. (p. 80)

Many societies legitimate—or perhaps even mandate—nonmarital sexual involvements (Wade, 1993). But accounts of host-culturally legiti-mate sexual participation have been made by male rather than by female

28

field-workers (reflecting either conduct or conduct norms differentiated by gender). Among the Mbuti of Africa studied by Colin Turnbull (1986), sexual conduct was a topic of lively interest because it signaled not only marital intentions but also one's place in the system of gender and age relationships. During his episodic research among the Mbuti, Turnbull reports that as a male, he was expected to engage in sexual relations at some ages but not at others. As an adopted child and later as an elder, Turnbull was defined culturally as asexual, but during the middle years of youth and young adulthood, when sexual nonparticipation was characteristic only of sorcerers, he was expected to engage in sexual behavior. He describes the temporary sexual and emotional arrangement he made during this stage with a woman, Amina, which "satisfied the Mbuti as to the normality of my youthfulness and my ability to continue to live with them as a real youth, while it satisfied the villagers that I was not a sorcerer" (Turnbull, 1986, p. 25). Turnbull also describes several fieldwork occasions when he refrained from sex

> when, as a philosophy graduate student with no training at all in anthropology I found myself in bed, in India, with a very attractive young Hindu girl who, because she called me brother, expected nothing more [as did her parents] but tickling contests, I was able to respond in kind with a minimum of difficulty. . . . Similarly, having studied anthropology and on my way to the field for my first professional fieldwork, there was a natural rightness about the insistence of an extremely powerful Ndaka chief that I sleep with one of his daughters. But here I was in trouble, this time for medical rather than moral reasons, for I was simply not willing to take the risk: the old chief and his entire family were ridden with leprosy and yaws, as well as syphilis. (p. 19)

Peter Wade (1993) is concerned with the racial and internationalist-political as well as gendered and sexual meanings of relationships in the field, a focus common to ethnographic methodology of the 1990s. In describing his "two quite long term" relationships with "local black Colombian women" during two periods of fieldwork in Columbia, he took note of the global meanings of such gendered, sexualized encounters for "processes of social mobility and cultural change . . . imbued with ambiguous but powerful meanings both of equality and hierarchy" (Wade, 1993, p. 200). In entering into the two sexual relationships, Wade mirrored his own masculinity within the "social representation of masculinity" in his setting and found a place as "something other than an oddity, a pryer, or a snooper," in part through his sexual and intimate encounters (Wade, 1993, p. 208).

There are not many accounts of heterosexual activities in the field by men (see Goode, 1999), and there are even fewer by women. Dona Davis (1986) provides a circumspect account of her affair with an engineer who had come to help with the installation of a water system in the Newfoundland village she was studying. Because the norms of this Newfoundland community included a prohibition against premarital sex for women, she was worried about the effect that staying overnight with this man would have on her research. In fact, her behavior led to the discovery that this norm was not expected to actually govern conduct; in fact, "having a 'boyfriend' or being 'paired off' seemed to make people a bit friendlier and more at ease around me" (Davis, 1986, p. 254).

In both Western and non-Western cultures, some settings are more sexually focused than others; doing research in such settings inevitably implicates the researcher in sexual imputations. In her studies of three Micronesian cultures, for example, Fischer (1986, p. 277) found that there were no age limits beyond which an individual could have his or her motives suspected. Researchers in Western cultures have encountered similar suspicions when studying settings such as nude beaches (Douglas, Rasmussen, & Flanagan, 1977), massage parlors (Warren & Rasmussen, 1977), and the specifically sexual arenas (rather than, say, communities, identities, bars, or sociability) of homosexual, gay, lesbian, or bisexual settings[10] (Styles, 1979; Warren & Rasmussen, 1977).

But even in highly heterosexualized settings, Western social scientists tend to refer to others' imputations rather than to their own inclinations in their publications. Even in writing about settings where sexual activity is fairly public, field-workers have remained silent about their own sexual participation or lack of it. In describing his research in a massage parlor, Paul Rasmussen comments that this setting was both sexualized and differentiated by gender roles, with men as customers, parlor owners, and boyfriends of the masseuses and women as masseuses (who provided sexual services for a fee) and girlfriends. As an attractive, young, male researcher, Rasmussen threatened the males in the setting—the owners for financial reasons and the customers and boyfriends for sexual reasons. He dealt with the latter problem by "secretly" disclosing that he was gay (he wasn't). Some of the masseuses, on the other hand, wanted him as a boyfriend and consequently—he suspected—downplayed their sexual involvement in the massage scene when he interviewed them. He countered this problem by bringing in a woman colleague to interview the masseuses. Throughout his discussion of these research problems, Rasmussen does not mention his own sexual activities or lack of them (Warren & Rasmussen, 1977, p. 363).

The nude beaches explored by Rasmussen and other research team members were, like the massage parlors he studied, a sexual setting, although its gender relations seemed more egalitarian. He comments that

> the nude beach scene is one of considerable sexual tension and display, although not necessarily in the form of overt sexual encounters. Newcomers to the scene hear a rhetoric of naturalism and freedom, while more seasoned participants learn to understand and negotiate the less apparent sexual dimensions of the scene. (Warren & Rasmussen, 1977, p. 364)

Women and men team members found that people on the nude beach told them different things. Single men told Rasmussen about their sexual interests but provided the woman researcher (Flanagan) only with the rhetoric of freedom and naturalism. The reverse was true when single women were interviewed by either Rasmussen or Flanagan. When only one interviewer was used to interview couples on the beach, the issue of jealousy arose, so they learned to interview couples jointly (Warren & Rasmussen, 1977, pp. 364-365).

In less (hetero) sexualized Western settings, sociologists have been even more reticent about sex. Writing of his fieldwork in a social welfare office in Southern California in the late 1960s, John Johnson notes the absence of reported sexual activity between respondents and field-workers in methodological accounts, then comments on his own affair with a social worker-informant in the field. This affair, he adds, "produced a severe crisis for me personally and delayed the writing of the research reports" (Johnson, 1975, p. 166). Yet the affair did not, apparently, affect Johnson's place in the social welfare office he was studying because in most settings in Western society, sex is defined as a private activity without a ritual place in organizational work and public life.[11]

The arena of ethnographic research in which there is the most common expression of sexual interest and participation is in the area of homosexuality—but again, this is more true of males than of females. One root of the disclosure motif is the transition made by some homosexual individuals and groups from secrecy to overtness, a process that had its beginning in the gay liberation movement of the 1960s. The other is the nature of the gay world itself: a subculture in which sexuality and social order are fused, linking sexual activities and preferences to lifestyle, leisure, and—increasingly—work (including ethnographic work).

Among the earliest sociological accounts of homosexual participation during field research is Joe Styles's (1979) "Insider/Outsider: Researching Gay Baths," a thoughtful analysis of the epistemology of participation and exclusion in ethnographic work. During his research in gay baths, he went from an outsider to the sexual activities in the baths to a sexual participant (although his identity as a gay man remained the same throughout). He concludes that neither the insider myth (that only inside participation can reveal truth) nor the outsider myth (of objectivity-as-discovery) is a useful way of seeing ethnographic work. He comments,

> Insider and outsider myths are not empirical generalizations about the relationship between the researcher's social position and the character of the research findings. They are elements in a moral rhetoric that claims exclusive research legitimacy for a particular group. . . . In reference to my own field work, the validity of this . . . point should be self-evident. I did not possess any special access to the life of the baths merely because I am gay. . . . And even when I became a real insider, I still made errors. . . . If, as an insider, I did have some strange epistemologically privileged position, I cannot point to any of its manifestations, for I continued to make erroneous assumptions throughout the course of my field work. (Styles, 1979, pp. 148-149)

Nevertheless, in general within the literature on ethnographic methods, the researcher's sexual activity (if any) in the setting remains "in the closet." And, as noted in the first edition of *Gender Issues,* this is even more true of women's than of men's sexual activity. As Caplan (1993a) notes of the fieldwork literature, more authors than in previous volumes (such as Golde, 1970/1986; Whitehead & Conaway, 1986) talk about sex, though deafening silences remain:

> While all three men consider this topic . . . only one of the women . . . is courageous enough to discuss it at any length and no woman acknowledges a sexual experience in the field. . . . The silence in the literature with reference to [homosexuality] is even more deafening than that concerning heterosexual relationships. (Caplan, 1993a, p. 23)

If the fieldwork literature on mutual sexual attraction and sexual episodes seems to be predominantly a male one, the literature on sexual danger is predominantly a female one. The issue of danger in the field, linked with the potential of violence among men, has sexualized aspects in the

1990s as it did in the 1930s. Fieldwork done by Liz Brunner among the homeless of Los Angeles illustrates the contemporary salience of the problem of women's safety in the field.[12] During her fieldwork, Brunner slept, drank, talked, and shared meals with the homeless on Los Angeles streets—almost all of whom were male. After several episodes of unwanted physical touching, she learned to avoid being alone with particular men or going into dark areas of the street with those she did not know well. Like villagers in a primitive culture, these homeless men—some of them deinstitutionalized mental patients—often did not share or perhaps did not know about Brunner's Western middle-class, feminist values and beliefs concerning sexual expression and male-female relationships. Terry Williams and her colleagues note that in their urban project and in other settings,

> Several female ethnographers have had their fieldwork severely constrained or have had to terminate it completely . . . due to the sexual expectations and demands of subjects or other males in the research setting. The threat of sexual assault or rape is a real concern for most female ethnographers and staff members. (Williams, Dunlap, Johnson, & Hamid, 1992, p. 363)

Women sociologists in ostensibly nonsexualized Western settings—from courtrooms to hospital wards—have over the years reported encounters with respondents, often key informants, characterized by various forms of sexual harassment. Sometimes these interactions take the form of overt sexual propositions (Rovner-Piecznik, 1976), but more often women report overpersonalization of interaction (Warren, 1982) or the sexual hustle disguised as research cooperation (Gurney, 1985, p. 48).

Accounts of sexual touching are found not so much in the published literature as in the oral fieldwork folklore. One anthropological exception is Mary Ellen Conaway's (1986, p. 59) discussion of her fieldwork as a single woman among the Guahibo Indians of Venezuela, during which she was not only asked if she would have sex for money but was also physically molested:

> I was mapping and identifying house types. . . . In the course of this work I met a Guahibo man, around sixty years of age, who delighted in sharing with me his life story and the history of the region. His wife had died a year earlier. . . . I departed ebullient—my first informant? After our third session, when I rose to depart, he extended his slight, four-foot-ten-inch frame, and, quick as

lightning, rubbed his nose across my clavical [sic]. I left disturbed. Future quick movement on my part prevented repetition of his affectionate behavior. (Conway, 1986, p. 55)

During her interview research with divorced men, Arendell (1997) reports not only episodes of verbal harassment but also physical harassment ranging from personal space violations to actual touching. She reports that numerous men touched her on the back, shoulder, hand, wrist, or arm, often when making a point in their responses. More blatantly sexualized episodes also occurred; for instance, one man adjusted his body increasingly closer to hers during the interviews, and another attempted to put his arm around her while offering to "warm her up" when she shivered as she departed into a cool evening. Other episodes were more aggressive. She reports that one man tapped the center of her chest to indicate where on his body he had been hit by his ex-wife. In a quite dramatic instance, during an interview at a restaurant, Arendell tells us,

> As he recalled how he had picked up his estranged wife by the neck, causing her to struggle, choke, and gag, he thrust his arm across the table and put his hand around my neck. . . . I pushed my chair back as far as it would go, but quickly hit up against the wall and so was trapped within his reach. . . . Not until the fourth time hearing the tape did I realize that a waitress had approached the table and asked if everything was ok. She did so at about the time the man removed his hand from next to my face. . . . At no time did the interviewee seem aware that I was shaken by this incident. I was surprised, and relieved, when I didn't develop bruises on my neck. (pp. 360-361)

Conaway, Arendell, Brunner, and other women who have been sexually harassed in the field have generally reported responding with evasive rather than confrontive action. Terry Williams, in her urban ethnographic work, notes that when she encounters sexualized interaction on the part of men, "Usually I just move away or shift to a conversation with someone else" (Williams et al., 1992, p. 355). Even with the more aggressive behaviors Arendell (1997) experienced, she states, "I mostly circumvented sexist innuendos and comments and continued conversing without confronting men's expressions of sexism or misogyny or inappropriate attentions" (p. 363). In reflecting on her hesitance to directly challenge these men, Arendell attributes her behavior to three primary considerations: First, "Had I responded critically in any way during my meetings with these volunteers, I would have prompted a different study than the one conducted" (p. 364). Because the purpose of her research was to explore divorce experiences of men, it was these accounts she was committed to attending to, rather than trying to "educate them to my way of seeing things, raise their consciousness . . . or attempt to dispel inaccurate assertions about divorce in the contemporary United States" (p. 363). Another reason she provides concerns her empathic involvement with respondents' accounts during the interviews. During the actual interview interactions, she found herself caught up in men's stories and agreeing with what she later perceived as illogical claims or mistaken beliefs. Third, a confrontational stance conflicted with the gratitude Arendell felt toward respondents: "I appreciated these men's voluntary participation in the study. They gave generously of their time and energy" (p. 364). Such low-key responses may frequently be part of the field-worker's general "gratitude" standpoint toward her or his respondents. Indeed, this gratitude may be one reason that "corridor talk" has noted many more instances of sexual harassment and other problematic behaviors among respondents than is inscribed by field-workers (Warren, 1980).

The literature on sexual danger is one of female victims and male predators, and it is a heterosexual narrative. The predatory male is also depicted in other discussions of gendered danger; when males are victims, the danger lies in physical rather than sexual assault. However, Terry Williams and her colleagues also note that violence is a potential danger to both women and men in contemporary urban research[13] (Williams et al., 1992, p. 366). Hopper and Moore (1990), in their research on women in outlaw motorcycle gangs, note that their respondents' slogan was "One good fist is worth a thousand words"; thus, it was "too dangerous to take issue with outlaws on their own turf" (pp. 368-370). Myers (1992, p. 270) notes that he shared the immediate danger of (not from) his respondents, whose lifestyles meant the constant threat of harm.

We can conclude from examining the field research literature on sexuality that its pervasiveness (Johnson, 1975) is not always reflected in the themes on which we as ethnographers like to elaborate. We can also conclude, we think, something about the sex and gender norms of our own culture from reading the fieldwork literature. It is the male social scientists who write about the pervasiveness and power of sexuality in a general rather than contextual or relational sense (see, e.g., Johnson, 1975; Turnbull, 1986). And it is the male social scientists (still only a minority, of course, of all male social scientists) who tell us about their sexual experiences in the field. Whitehead and Price (1986) note that the imbalance in treating sexuality issues . . . does not necessarily mean that these difficulties are more prevalent for male than for female fieldworkers. . . . There is a double taboo at work—sanctions against discussing sexuality publicly, particularly for women, and . . . sanctions . . . against public acknowledgment of factors that might undermine objectivity in the field. (p. 294)

Women social scientists, in contrast to men, seem more likely to inscribe sexual harassment and danger, rather than their own sexual desires, and stress marriage offers rather than proposals of a less licit nature. The one partial exception is the lesbian and gay fieldwork literature in which both women and men speak of their sexual relationships—but the women, still, more circumspectly, within disembodiments of community and identity (see, e.g., Esterberg, 1997). The discourse of sexuality, in our culture, is one subsumed within the more general discourse of gender.

3. INTERVIEWING AND GENDER: STUDYING UP CLOSE AND FAR APART

Ethnography and interviewing, although epistemologically rather different (Harkess & Warren, 1993; Warren, 1987), are in practice used as supplements or replacements for traditional fieldwork (Holstein & Gubrium, 1995). Conversation is part of almost any field; formalized and fixed on the audio or visual recording device, they become the "intensive," "active," "long," or "ethnographic" interview. Interviews may also stand alone, to provide data on topics for which there is no (accessible) setting but rather shared experiences or because the setting cannot readily be entered by the researcher.

Like the field-worker who may strive to take a stance of distance or immersion, interviews are used across the whole range of ethnographic distance. For Western anthropologists, the interview may decrease distance (e.g., to clarify the kin structures of non-Western peoples); on the other hand, in those research situations in which the ethnographer studies her or his "own people," it may bring distance between self and respondent.

Interviews are also similar to traditional fieldwork in that the stance we take and the relationships we form are not strictly under our control but rather a process of interaction and negotiation. As such, interviewers may find themselves cast in the roles discussed above or, especially in the single-shot interview with a stranger, some variant of the above roles. For instance, although in the lone interview, a respondent is unlikely to view a researcher as (fictive) kin, the researcher may get cast as "confidante" or "best friend." Likewise, the honorary male role, in a temporally and spatially limited encounter, can become the "expert" or "authority."

Lofland and Lofland (1984, p. 38) suggest that qualitative researchers attempt to take a stance of the "socially acceptable incompetent"—someone who is friendly and likable yet who needs help in understanding the basics of things. But as noted previously, despite a researcher's attempts to take a role, informants actively engage in imposing a role on the researcher. In researching issues of the body and social control, Hackney (1995, 1998) often found that the role she was assigned varied not according to topic or culture (as all interviewees were Westerners) but according to how she and respondents "matched" on various characteristics. Among young, adult, middle-class women similar to herself, Hackney often found herself placed in the role of confidante. However, among similar men, she often felt cast as "expert" or "authority." Although this role is somewhat akin to the "honorary male" role, it seems that most literature on the honorary male role claims that this status affords women increased access to the worlds of men. In contrast, when cast as the expert interviewer, Hackney found access more difficult—informants would provide brief and succinct responses, peppered with expressions of concern about providing "correct" responses or requests for information regarding the "facts" found in her own or other research. Another type of questioning would occur when Hackney was occasionally cast in the "child" role. This seemed to occur when the informant was substantially older or higher in the professional hierarchy than Hackney. In these cases, the roles of interviewer-interviewee seemed to become reversed, as informants would quiz Hackney, as well as provide active instruction on topics such as additional reading, Hackney's interview style, and theoretical perspectives. Simultaneously, however, these interviews were characterized by a sense of trust, openness, and sincere helpfulness such as the type offered to children in our society.

This sense of candor, trust, and helpfulness in interviews in which the researcher is cast as a child is very different from when one is cast in the role of a different type of inferior. In her article on unmatched gender interviewing, Terry Arendell (1997) not only interviewed men but also interviewed them about their own divorces. She found that the divorce experience had highlighted "the issue of their identity *as men* which, in their views, had been brought into question by their divorce experiences"

(Arendell, 1997, p. 347). Arendell found that from the initial point of contact, the interview became a proving ground for masculinity and a site for the exercise of male definitions and dominance displays against ex-wives (and sometimes against all women). Unlike a similar earlier study of mothers, these men immediately "took charge" of the interview process and topic, "leading the conversational dance" throughout. Both by asking questions and by making assumptions, the respondents attempted to "place" Arendell as married or unmarried, available or not, male basher or nice girl. Their "assertion of superiority" involved both the denigration of women in general and the assumption of superior knowledge and insights on the part of them than Arendell. Their handling of the interview (for it was they that handled) ranged from chivalry to, at least in one case, sexual harassment[14] (Arendell, 1997).

Gender is implicated in interviewing as in ethnography. In addition to women interviewing men or women, men may interview women or men, and there can be group, focus, or triadic interviews beyond the dyad. Although there is much less information on gender in ethnographic interviewing than on ethnographic fieldwork, there is some—both prescriptive and descriptive. And, as in other discussions and recommendations in the methodological literature, shifts have occurred in what is inscribed as ideal. The early Chicago school interviewing literature was, like the ethnographic or case study, premised on the interviewer as "any person." In a section on "The Interview as a Social Situation," Vivien Palmer, in her canonical 1928 text on *Field Studies in Sociology*, indicated that

> any interview constitutes a social interaction between two individuals; it is a process of continuous, spiral interaction in which one person's response to the stimulation of another in turn becomes the stimulation for another response. (pp. 170-171)

Palmer (1928) goes on to discuss the balance between keeping the respondent focused and allowing her to tell a story, having rapport, and recording the interview in the respondent's "natural language"—including the use of "dicographs" or "motion picture machines" (p. 177). She mentions types of interview, training interviewers, contacting stranger-respondents, and terminating the interview. At no point, however, does she mention the gender (or during this era, more properly, "sex") of either the respondent or the interviewer.

The interviewer with "no gender" (like the ethnographer as "any person") ceded place during the century to the male interviewer interviewing both women and men (Kinsey's model—see Davidson & Layder, 1994) and the matched interview, with respondent and researcher matched on gender and other personal characteristics such as race and age. During the modern era, accounts of what made an interview go smoothly and produce valid data were contested terrain: any polite and dignified interviewer (Palmer, 1928), a male interviewer (Cressey, 1986), or a female interviewer with a female respondent (Oakley, 1981). The contemporary positivist literature prescribes the "match" of interviewer and respondent by age, race, and gender—and perhaps as many other characteristics as money and hiring practices make possible. But the terrain of contest has widened even further during recent years.

In postmodern times, the gendered interview has been rewritten in the context of the meaning of the interviewer and interview topic to both respondent and researcher during the "interview (still) as social interaction." Both Palmer (1928) and Kinsey (see Davidson & Layder, 1994) envisioned the interview as interaction between strangers; today's focus on "starting where you are" has given rise to many more situations in which the respondent and interview are part of the same social circles, even intimates (Harkess & Warren, 1993; see also Krieger, 1986). And among both intimates and strangers, when the topic as well as the interviewer is gendered, sexualized, or both, then the research interview is fraught with interactional possibilities.

Currently, "women interviewing women" is a "match" often framed in the literature as involving "no problems." Even with the widening of the debate of who should interview whom during the postmodern era, the female dyad is often deproblematized. Since the work of Ann Oakley (1981), Marjorie DeVault (1986), and others on feminist interviewing, the dyad of a feminist woman interviewing another woman has been valorized, even perhaps romanticized, as the ideal research relationship. When, however, the matched-gender dyad is also sexualized, as in the case of Susan Krieger's (1986) research with fellow lesbians, then problems may be admitted to the narrative.

One of the few accounts of heterosexual women interviewing heterosexual women that we found that did not insist on unproblematic rapport was Rosanna Hertz's (1996) study of the views of military men and their wives concerning gender integration in the military. Not unexpectedly, Hertz found that the men interviewed by the two women interviewers were sometimes uncomfortable trying "to explain . . . their position to people who were outsiders to male camaraderie" (p. 256). Like Arendell (1997), Hertz also noticed that the men respondents sometimes framed the interviewers as representing the views of all women. But in addition, they noted that the women respondents had even less to say than the men and surmised that their shared status as women was overshadowed by differences of education, marital status, and social class between the interviewers and the respondents (Hertz, 1996, p. 256).

4. GENDER AND REPRESENTATION

As indicated earlier, accounts of sex and gender in the field may be framed in the language of rapport, or they may be analyzed epistemologically. In this section, methodological accounts are taken *as* accounts, to be read for that web of gender that occurs in the production of discourse rather than in the recounting of anecdotes. The contemporary epistemology of gender in social science has moved from analytic concerns with feminist theory (about settings) to rhetorical concerns with discourse analysis (about the transformation of settings into knowledge through social science categories) and the reading of fieldwork documents—from field notes to ethnographies—as literary texts.

There is a lack of explicit connection in our and in others' methodological accounts between anecdotes of the field, on one hand, and presentational strategies, on the other. We are told, for example, that Carolyn Fleuhr-Lobban, as a married woman, was treated to oil massages, and we are told that rapport was enhanced for Dona Davis (1986) by taking a lover. The implication—sometimes the explicit indication—is that the events described in these anecdotes resulted in greater rapport, which in turn resulted in access to more (and presumably more truthful) information. Besides the very real possibility that there may be situations in which tension, conflict, and a lack of rapport might produce more (truthful) information, what is missing in this interactionist sequence is the semiotic: the process through which interactions are reproduced as knowledge—as analytic categories, as field notes, as ethnographies. Instead of weaving connections between experience and the production of knowledge, recently, ethnographers tend to produce and maintain various mythologies, including that of women's place in fieldwork methodology.

Women's Place in Fieldwork "Mythodology"

Just as women are defined as occupying certain specific and gendered places in a given culture, they appear in the fieldwork literature in particu-

lar ways. And the ways that women are portrayed have changed over time. To illustrate, we want to consider briefly the place of gender in the methodological accounts of the Chicago school field-workers, using as an illustration a 1920s essay by Paul Cressey (published in 1986). In the fieldwork (or case study) literature of the first Chicago school, neither gender nor many other methodological issues were seen as especially problematic.[15] Cressey typically discusses gender only in the more general context of research role. Using a theoretical framework derived from Simmel's (1950) analysis of the stranger, Cressey describes the relationships he and other members of his research team (a White woman and a Filipino man) experienced in the taxi dance halls they were studying. As in Simmel's original analysis, Cressey's stranger seems to be, both implicitly and explicitly, a male stranger. As Cressey put it,

> Simmel lays particular emphasis upon the fact that the stranger is a product of mobility in that he is physically present yet culturally distant from the group—and yet a part of it. Likewise, Simmel emphasizes the enhanced freedom from sentiment and the folkways and mores of the group, and the increased objectivity that results. . . . But the contribution of Simmel to our specific problem is found in a special suggestion of his. He points out that in the relation of the stranger to the group he has opportunity to gain surprising confessional rapport with the others of the community. (Cressey, 1986, p. 104)

Grammatically, the stranger is "he." Although this may have been the standard grammatical format of the time, historically, Simmel's (1950) analysis was developed in the context of a society in which the strangers who were becoming commonplace in society were male traders and migrants thrown on the shores of urbanization and modernization. But Simmel's and Cressey's (1986) ideal typical stranger also partakes epistemologically of many traits associated with maleness (Keller, 1985): freedom from sentiment and independence from the mores and folkways, as well as objectivity within a web of subjectivity. Ironically, that characteristic of the stranger portrayed as most useful to understanding the methodology of fieldwork is one associated in the contemporary fieldwork literature with femaleness—the ability to communicate and gain confessional rapport.

Cressey's (1986) essay alerts us to the possibility that this view of women's special place in fieldwork may be more a feature of discourse than a social fact. He saw the male bond, rather than the characteristics associated with women, as the basis for a confessional relation between the sociological stranger and his respondent, commenting that

> it may be said that the anonymous confessional relationship is a monosexual grouping. Its most striking instance is in the relationship of two men, although to a lesser extent the same dyadic grouping may exist between two women. Such anonymous confidential relationship may exist between a man and a woman, although perhaps less frequently and less completely. (p. 110)

Cressey (1986) provides some details about gender and its intersection with ethnicity in the taxi dance hall research, supporting his general hypothesis concerning fieldwork rapport and the male bond. He worked with a young woman student to try to gain interview rapport with the taxi dance hall hostesses, but

> before long it was apparent that she could not establish rapport with the girls. She might engage them in a brief conversation, but none of the girls were interested in continuing these confidences. (Cressey, 1986, p. 112)

Although he attributes the lack of rapport in part to the woman researcher's moralizing attitude, Cressey (1986) assumes unproblematically that men are more likely to achieve rapport with respondents than women.

Cressey (1986) also collaborated with a male Filipino coworker whom he used to gain interviews with the male Filipino clientele of the taxi dance hall. Although this young man was able to talk to the Greek (male) proprietors of the dance halls—who were in general prejudiced against Filipinos—they would talk only about money and their ownership, not about the girls. Sexual topics were taboo between the representatives of what were then defined as more and less stigmatized ethnic groups (Cressey, 1986, p. 108). Despite Cressey's recognition of the difficulties faced by his male collaborator, he maintains his assumptions regarding the superior abilities of men to achieve rapport.

Cressey's (1986) views regarding gender and communication contrast sharply with contemporary wisdom on the issue. Since the 1920s, the special features and problems of women's place in culture and in fieldwork have given rise to a mythology of women's particular contributions to the fieldwork enterprise. This special place assigned to women is based on women's general social place as nurturers, communicators, emotional laborers, and (as a muted undertone) sexual objects. It is almost a truism in the methodological literature of interview research, for example, that in most situations women will be able to achieve more rapport with respondents because of their less threatening quality and better communication skills. Male interviewers are generally considered preferable only for highly restricted topics such as police work and then only in relation to male respondents.

Although women may sometimes be prevented from entering male social worlds, they are depicted nevertheless as encountering more willingness from both females and males to be allowed access to the inner worlds of feeling and thought. Female field-workers are seen simultaneously as less threatening and more open to emotional communication than men (Codere, 1986; Golde, 1970/1986; Macintyre, 1993; Whitehead & Conaway, 1986). Both in sociology and in anthropology, fieldwork has been associated with women and quantitative work with men. Laura Nader (1986) summarizes,

> Women make a success of field work because women are more person-oriented; it is also said that participant observation is more consonant with the traditional role of women. Like many folk explanations there is perhaps some truth in the idea that women, at least in Western culture, are better able to relate to people than men are. (p. 114)

This portrayal contrasts sharply with Cressey's 1920s assumptions of the male dyad as being the most intimate and open form of relationship. Although Cressey was also a member of Western culture, he studied the taxi dance halls during a time when men were believed to be superior in forming social relationships and achieving relational rapport.

Both the ideology of better communication skills and a trading in female sexuality are, we think, implicated in the mythology of women field-workers' use as "sociability specialists," opening up situations and respondents and generally smoothing the path for male members of fieldwork teams. In their study of the nude beach (Douglas et al., 1977), Douglas and Rasmussen eventually employed Carol Ann Flanagan, a woman they met on the beach, as a "sociability specialist" and coauthor. As Douglas (1979) comments,

> In most settings, the ultimate sociability specialists are women. These low-key women do not threaten either the women or the men. They are liked by and commonly share intimacies with both sexes. Men are simply more threatening to both sexes, even when they are the most sociable. (p. 214)

43

This blend of the nurturing and sexual facets of women's place in culture and in fieldwork is particularly evident in settings where sexuality is a focus (the nude beach, the massage parlor) but is also relevant to settings, such as formal organizations, where sexuality remains an undercurrent to the bureaucratic business at hand. In Warren's (1982) research in the mental health court, she found that the judge's sponsorship of her and his willingness to share information with her—and indeed force her presence on others in the setting, which he had the power to do—were premised almost entirely on his wish to engage in daily flirtations. Warren was a sexualized mascot not only to this aging judge but also to several other men in the setting, who were pleased to parade in and out of the courtrooms and chambers with her in a tow.

The generalizations found in the social science literature concerning the advantages and disadvantages of women versus men in fieldwork also reflect women's place in their own social order. Besides their restriction to particular worlds within settings, women field-workers are portrayed as more accessible and less threatening than men; coupled with women's presumed superior communicative abilities, the interactions of fieldwork are generally depicted as easier for women than men (Fischer, 1986; Golde, 1970/1986; Mead, 1986; Warren & Rasmussen, 1977; Wax, 1979). Furthermore, although the field-workers who write about the different experiences of women and men are careful to note that these generalizations depend on the purposes and methods of the study, the host culture, and the other characteristics of the field-worker (such as age and marital status), these portrayals exhibit a remarkable cross-cultural similarity. From Greenland to New Guinea and from New England in the 1960s to Los Angeles in the 1970s, women (we are told) achieve better rapport with people.

OBJECTIVITY AND EMOTIONS IN FIELD RESEARCH

In addition to better rapport with informants, the "modernist" literature also portrays women making a special contribution to fieldwork through bringing back into focus the emotional as well as cognitive aspects of social research. As Evelyn Fox Keller (1985) points out, science has been historically identified with rationality, objectivity, cognition, and the mistrust of emotion—traits also associated with men. Women, on the other hand, have been identified with irrationality, subjectivity, and emotionality, all anathema to proper science and social science. It is within fieldwork and the development of an ethnographic tradition that the emotional and the cognitive dimensions of social research have become an important focus of scholarly attention.

Social scientists have increasingly come to take seriously the presumption that findings and methods are interdependent and that feelings as well as ideas guide research design, procedures, relationships, and analysis. The day-to-day work of research in any setting involves feelings of like and dislike, boredom and annoyance, fear and shame. And some research brings the researcher face to face with profound experiences of birth or death, aging or pain. Barbara Katz Rothman (1986), for example, describes the guilt and grief associated with her research on amniocentesis and abortion in the context of her own recent motherhood:

> I had no idea how much pain was there, or how much pain I would suffer. . . . I was so close, emotionally and physically, to the pregnancy experience, to the terrible, urgent intimacy of that relationship. And [my] baby—I loved her so passionately, so fiercely. . . . It was partly survivors' guilt. . . . The constant going back and forth between these women and their grief . . . and my love from my healthy baby—it tore at me, but it made me try to understand the meaning of mother love. (pp. 50-52)

These profound emotions changed the course of Rothman's (1986) research. She came to interpret amniocentesis and abortion not simply as medical events but as the death of a baby, with all the pain that entails for a woman and mother. She eventually hired a research assistant—a young woman who had no children—to continue the interviewing with those whose amniocentesis had resulted in an abortion.

Although the consequences of Rothman's (1986) emotions began while she was still gathering data, it was not until following the publication of *Fisher Folk* that Carolyn Ellis experienced such intense emotion that she felt compelled to alter the course of her research (Ellis, 1995a; see also Allen, 1997). The publication of this ethnography provoked the wrath of her informants, causing her to feel deep remorse and reevaluate the connections between self and other, between emotion and knowledge in orthodox ethnography (Ellis, 1995a). She later moved her main appointment from sociology to communications, and her more recent projects involve the use of auto-ethnography as a technique. In *Final Negotiations* (Ellis, 1995b), she details the intimacies of her relationship with Eugene Weinstein, a fellow sociologist, who died of emphysema in 1985. She shares with readers her and Weinstein's experiences with drugs, sex, and illness. In contrast with her earlier ethnography of the fishing community in Virginia, she came to include her own emotions as a central point for analysis in her research.

In the social science of the 1920s through the 1950s, a stance of objectivity and rationality was still the aim of field-workers as well as of more statistically oriented social scientists (Thomas, 1983). Indeed, older social scientists, such as Margaret Mead, writing in their later years, cautioned against what they saw as the increasing emotionalism of the field in general, particularly women (Mead, 1986). The proper expression of feelings was not in the published ethnography or even in the field notes but in such private texts as diaries and letters; even there, the expression of feelings could provoke dismay, as did Malinowski's private diaries when they were published in 1967 (Mead, 1986, pp. 324, 324n). Today, however, there has been a renewed substantive and methodological interest in the role of emotions in social life, which has resulted in the reevaluation of the interrelationship of gender, feeling, and rationality in science and social science (Bendelow & Williams, 1998; Ellis, 1995b; Hochschild, 1983; Keller, 1985). Although debates continue to exist on the "appropriateness" of this interest, in social science, as in social life, a focus on emotions is associated with women.

Feminism, Postmodernism, and Ethnography as Representation

Since the 1980s, the issue of representation has come to the forefront of interdisciplinary discourses on the making of ethnographic and other texts. And the framework for understanding representation has been either feminist, postmodernist, or both. Building on the work of scholars such as Strathern (1984), Gusfield (1976), and Clifford and Marcus (1986), feminist and postmodern ethnographers have sought to deconstruct and reconstruct the ways in which ethnographers represented their gendered (and racialized) subjects.

It is not that the gender of representation went unnoticed prior to the 1980s; since the 1920s, it has generally been women ethnographers who came to recognize the implicit assumption that what is important about society is what the men are up to. From her research on Pacific cultures in the 1930s and 1940s, anthropologist Camilla Wedgwood (1957) concluded,

It is sometimes assumed unwittingly that the males play the dominant role in social change and that for a study of acculturation the effects of culture contact on the females are relatively unimportant. The effects on the lives and outlooks of the females are less obvious, less direct, and usually less easy to analyze, but we cannot assume that they are less important. (p. 495)

Anthropologists and sociologists of the 1980s and 1990s researched the male bias in the discipline, using the work of canonical male anthropologists as examples or prompting the reexamination of the submerged women in the field (Fraser, 1989; O'Brien, 1989; Parezo, 1993a; Sprague, 1993). Annette Weiner challenges Malinowski's interpretation of Trobriand Island culture:

> Weiner believes that Malinowski, like other scholars, places too much emphasis on individualistic and utilitarian concerns—for example the seeking of political alliance and power—and consequently neglected systems of exchange that involve women and are related to a society's sense of intergenerational community. . . . There is a great deal of truth in what Malinowski says, observed Weiner, but he was trapped by his own sense of what women were about. (Sass, 1986, p. 56)

What Malinowski "overlooked" was the meaning and significance of women's activity as cultural ritual, something that he saw only in male activity. Malinowski and others had established the importance of reciprocal gift exchanges in the public life of Trobriand Islanders but had assumed that Trobriand women made no such exchanges because they were confined to the domestic sphere. By contrast, Weiner described a female exchange ritual that she represented as "a linchpin [sic] of Trobriand social and cultural life" (Sass, 1986, p. 57).

Similar challenges to the prevailing definition of the situation have been made by contemporary feminist sociologists. The basic presuppositions of sociological theories, derived historically from a philosophical tradition, are gendered presuppositions—as Evelyn Fox Keller (1985) notes, it is, after all, White male Westerners who have been responsible for developing the language of philosophy and science. The classic sociologists—Marx, Weber, and Durkheim—all focused their theories around concepts of the division of labor that excluded the spheres particular to the women: their reproductive, household, and emotional labor. Both mainstream and Marxist sociology in the United States ignored the productive tasks of women partly because they were unpaid and partly because they took place in the domestic sphere. Not only the functionalist or Parsonian but even the critical or conflict theories of social order take male activities as their causal principle and as the source of social change.

Even today, however, ethnographic writers on both theory and methodology are likely to build their arguments on gendered presuppositions. Michael H. Agar (1986) describes the contribution made by the philosopher Alfred Schutz to the development of phenomenological and ethnographic perspectives:

> A person, living in a world endowed with meaning, has at any given moment an interest at hand. For our purposes, the interest at hand will be called a goal, of which the person may or may not be conscious. The goal of the moment is not an isolated entity; rather, it is part of a larger system of goals in a person's world. . . . The actor, with goal at hand, sketches out a plan of action based on anticipation and expectations in the stock of knowledge available. (p. 24)

Aside from the obvious Western cultural assumptions in Agar's (1986) rendition of Schutz (the notion of the unconscious, the systems perspective), the very emphasis on goals as the wellspring of social action seems to us to be premised on men's experience of the world—at least Western men whose generational membership spans roughly the era of Schutz to Agar. In a set of interviews Warren did as a graduate student, she investigated academic women's experience of their career trajectories. She was interested in finding out whether other women's experience had been like hers: characterized not so much by goals and planning but by drift and adjustment to circumstances. She found that for these late 1960s to early 1970s women professors, even the purportedly goal-organized career path of academia had indeed—and especially in the earlier stages—been characterized by drift and adaptation rather than goals, planning, and choice. They described entering graduate school in terms such as getting away from their household duties or having nothing else to do in the college town where their husbands had chosen to teach. We had been brought up to adapt to circumstances, often to men's plans, rather than to make plans and seek goals.[16]

Although the representations of ethnography are not free from the structuring of consciousness by social place (indeed, no representations are), field-workers have always been aware of the reflexive nature of knowledge. This awareness derives, we think, from the face-to-face nature of the method itself, which hinders the positivistic retreat into the myths of objectivity and "any person" research. Indeed, among the canons of the qualitative approaches in the social sciences are the unity of the knower and the known and the dependence of the findings on the procedures used in discovering. But it is only very recently that the significance

48

of gender and other aspects of reflexivity in the field has entered the main-stream of academic discourse and that fieldwork reflexivity has itself become the object of analysis. Attention in ethnography has turned to our own representations as they reveal the textual interaction of self and other.[17]

The postmodernist and/or feminist ethnography of the 1980s and 1990s (see, e.g., Bell, 1993; Lamphere et al., 1997; Strathern, 1984) engendered a concern with polyvocality: the presence of the voices of those dominated as well as those dominant—of respondents as well as ethnographers, women as well as men, people of color as well as Westerners. In *Situated Lives,* the editors note that

> the essays . . . throughout the collection demonstrate ways of writing that do not objectify our subjects. These include presenting women's voices in de-tail, paying attention to the variety among women's situations (rather than presenting one universal type of experience), and historically contextu-alizing ethnographic material. (Lamphere et al., 1997, p. 1)

Contemporary ethnographic representations by and about women stress a feminist commitment to mutual identification and engagement, amplified, during the 1990s, by a concern for globalization and racial issues as well as gender. The editors of *Situated Lives* set a structural and historical as well as interactional context for postmodern feminist ethnog-raphy by choosing works that

> illuminat[e] the lived experience of ordinary women and men. The essays we have selected focus on gender and culture, but they also place gender in rela-tion to the historical and material circumstances where gender, race, class, and sexual orientation intersect and shape everyday interaction. (Lamphere et al., 1997, p. 1)

But these new wisdoms of mutual, gendered identification and of poly-vocality have themselves been challenged by the incorporation of racial and global perspectives on gendered ethnography. In a trenchant critique of the postmodernist/feminist dominance in anthropological ethnogra-phy, Bell (1993) comments that

> the apparent isomorphism of these two fundamental critiques—feminist and postmodernist—of the ethnographic endeavor is at best illusory, at worst misleading. The "other" of postmodern writing is distanced from self by

geography, and by cultural, racial, and ethnic identity. It would appear that feminist critiques are more unsettling. They reveal that the "other" of the feminist—namely, the beneficiaries of patriarchy—are the very authors of the "new ethnography" who, under the guise of democratising ethnography through plurivocality, avoid scrutiny of their own power. By reducing ethnographic encounters to texts, the postmodernists have mystified the power of the ethnographer, and their experiments mask the location, and hence the ability of the author to structure and choose text and voice. . . . Yet the consequences of tracing a genealogy through women's reflections and experiments would be to position postmodernism not as a withering critique of the 1980s, but rather as a somewhat peevish, peripheral, self-interested, and in particular male construction. (Bell, 1993, p. 8)

Fieldwork Texts as Representations

Fieldwork accounts, despite Bell (1993), are often presented in ethnographic writing as representing not so much the setting as the interpretive moment; thus, gender is analyzed as it shapes not only the processes and presuppositions but also the productions of fieldwork. These productions include field notes, methodological accounts, and published research monographs and articles. In anthropology and in feminism, the use of others' field notes over time and a renewed attention to methodology have combined to produce an interest in field notes as text.[18]

Smith (1990, p. 2) notes somewhat cynically that the current concern with text, meaning, writing, and reflexivity is as much to be accounted for by its domination of Western intellectual life in the 1980s as by its relevance to the ethnographic enterprise per se, but he goes on to discuss his own use of the 40-year-old field notes of an anthropologist housewife. The exercise of using others' field notes, removed in time, place, and sometimes gender, has made anthropologists increasingly aware of their biographical and historical features. As Nancy Lutkehaus (1990) says of her use of Camilla Wedgwood's field notes from the 1930s,

My initial reading of [Wedgwood's] field journals and letters to friends, mentors and families . . . captivated my attention less for their data about Manam society and culture than for what they could tell me about Wedgwood herself. . . . Like Wedgwood, I was a woman going into the field alone, and easily identified with her . . . I tried to read between the lines . . . searching for clues in her account from forty-five years earlier as to what a similar experience might hold in store for me. (p. 313)

Lutkehaus not only used Wedgwood's field notes from the Manam research, but she also did her own fieldwork in New Guinea. She concludes that the differences she found in the culture could be explained not only by historical change between the 1930s and 1980s but also by the ways in which she and Wedgwood interpreted the interactions they observed. Where Wedgwood found the relationship between married women and men to be basically cooperative and harmonious, Lutkehaus saw it as fundamentally conflictful (Lutkehaus, 1982, pp. 36-41). She asks,

> How are we to reconcile these two disparate sets of information about male-female relations in Manam society? . . . Is Manam society accurately portrayed by the description of gender ideology but expresses difference but not dominance? (Lutkehaus, 1982, p. 41)

From a rhetorical or textual perspective, the locus of reconciliation would lie not in the nature of Manam society but in the biography and history of anthropological interpretation.

One of Warren's interests in the 1980s was the use of gender frameworks in ethnography in the context of historical and analytic changes within disciplines. In her study of schizophrenic women and their husbands in the 1950s (Warren, 1987), she used transcripts of interviews performed with institutionalized women and their husbands. This research prompted her to rethink Goffman's (1961) and other 1950s to 1970s ethnographies of mental hospitals, sick roles, and patienthood. The works from that period use essentially ungendered concepts and are ungendered texts. And yet we know that gender is visible to the observer—that Goffman, as he walked around the asylum, saw female and male mental patients. Warren, performing a document analysis, never actually saw the patients or staff she studied, and yet the gendered nature of recorded interactions appeared central to the institutional setting. Her analysis of the difference in gender focus between *Madwives* (Warren, 1987) and *Asylums* (Goffman, 1961) thus centers on the historical context in which these works were written. Although the intensive interview and fieldwork as methods may serve to differentially focus the researcher's attention, the differences between Goffman's text and Warren's stem primarily from being embedded in differing historical periods. Goffman was not, as Warren was, writing during a historical era when theories and their discourses were the subject of feminist analysis. To Goffman, gender is unproblematic. Likewise, in the transcripts of intensive interviews Warren used as data, the researchers performing the interviews also ignored the significance of gender in the construction of housewives as schizophrenic (however, the women interviewed would occasionally note their lack of conformity to prescribed roles as a cause or symptom of their insanity). During the time period in which Goffman wrote and the transcripts were created, the "naturalness" of women's roles and place was taken for granted. As an academic and a woman in the 1980s, by rereading these 1950s interview transcripts, the salience of gender to the moral career of the 1950s female mental patient was made quite clear through the lens of 1980s social science (see also DeVault, 1986; Kneeland & Warren, in press).

Field notes may be reinterpreted not only by others but also by the person who wrote them. Biographical change occurs in the context of historical change, and people come to think differently about their own interpretations. Anthropologists such as Caplan (1993b) and Wolf (1990) have explored the ways in which biographical changes have intersected with visits to the "same" field to produce reinterpretations of former representations of that field. In describing her fieldwork to an island off the coast of Tanzania, even the subheadings of Caplan's biographical account speak historical, disciplinary volumes: "The First Trip, 1965-7: Ungendered Field, Ungendered Self"; "Second Visit, 1976: Women in the Field, Woman in the Field"; and "Third Visit, 1985: Gender Problematised" (Caplan, 1993b, pp. 168-176).

Wolf (1990), in describing her field research in China as an anthropologist's wife in the 1950s and her later reinterpretation of her own field notes, notes the ways in which biographical and historical change result in different understandings of the same document. As did Ella Embree in Japan (Smith, 1990), Wolf took notes for her husband, mainly on the life of the women, from which he was excluded. During the 1960s and 1970s, she underwent two transformations: She became an anthropologist and a feminist. These changes led her to what she calls an engendering of her earlier field notes and emerging awareness of the significance of the world of the women of China and of the nature of their power:

The Chinese family as an institution has been [characterized as] . . . a male-dominated structure. . . . The consensus seemed to be that Chinese women [were] . . . of minimal interest in examining the Chinese family's strengths, cycles or romance. . . . I was vaguely aware of the invisibility of women at the time of my first fieldwork in Taiwan, but since my relationship to academia at that time was purely marital, I was neither interested nor constrained by the all-male paradigm. I hung out with the women, as did all women, and the understanding I acquired on the family was theirs. When I began to write, I dutifully read the important books about the Chinese family, and then, turning to my fieldnotes, began the struggle at which I was ultimately defeated. (Wolf, 1990, p. 348)

Wolf's account of her China field notes gives us insight into the nature of the relationship between biography and interpretation in historical context. She notes that her analytic problems with the androcentric paradigm of the Chinese family were first vague because she—and the discipline— lacked guidelines in the 1950s for making a gender-based critique. Once she began working as an anthropologist rather than as the wife of one, and in the context of a resurgence of feminism, she was able to write in a new way about the women in the Chinese family.

Within anthropology, one celebrated instance of ethnographic reinterpretation is the Mead-Freeman controversy over Mead's (1923) book *Coming of Age in Samoa*. Taken not only as an ethnography of adolescence and sexual awakening among young girls in Samoa but also as an indictment of child-rearing practices in the United States, Mead's book depicts an adolescence characterized by harmony rather than conflict. A different Samoa is portrayed by Derek Freeman (1983) based on his fieldwork 15 years following the departure of Mead. In his book *Margaret Mead in Samoa: The Making and Unmaking of an Anthropological Myth,* Freeman (1983, pp. 240, 290) wrote that Mead was deliberately misled by her adolescent informants with counterfeit tales of casual love under the palm trees. Tiffany and Adams (1985) contrast Mead's and Freeman's interpretations of Samoan adolescence:

Whereas Mead found ease, cooperation and easy sex, Freeman found a pathology of conflict, violence and rape. Instead of a gentle upbringing within the secure warmth of an extended family, Freeman claimed that Samoan children are regularly subjected to harsh punishments by their parents. Instead of adolescent boys and girls exploring the innocent pleasures of sex, Freeman described a society in which girls and women are terrorized by the omnipresent fear of brutal rape. (p. 27)

The fact that the Mead-Freeman debate was between a woman and a man has led other anthropologists to interpret these divergent accounts in a gendered context. First, the changes in the gender structure of Samoan society between Mead's and Freeman's visits perhaps provoked differential interpretation. Second, Freeman sought out, whereas Mead avoided, the male world of elite politics; Mead sought out, whereas Freeman avoided, the world of women and children (Tiffany & Adams, 1985). But Mead's and Freeman's differences in their accounts of those occasions on which men and women come together in sexual and family interactions indicate that their entrée into separate worlds of gender is not the only factor in their interpretive conflict. Tiffany and Adams (1985) suggest that Mead and Freeman were operating from within different anthropological allegories. Mead's text is infused with the pastoral or Edenic allegory of paradise lost (Clifford, 1986; Tiffany & Adams, 1985). Freeman, however, frames his in the dark allegory of the wild woman, as a powerless victim of savage lust, and Samoan women are depicted as brutalized sex objects, as well as violent aggressors:

> Samoan women are irrelevant in Freeman's analysis, except when they are duping Margaret Mead, punishing children, and fighting with other women over men. Samoan women are significant objects of scrutiny to Freeman the anthropologist when they are surreptitiously raped by sleep-crawlers, or manually deflowered by chiefs in public ceremonies. Terrorized by their male assailants who are obsessed by the cult of virginity . . . and fantasies of forcible defloration and rape, Samoan women are transformed into debased Wild Women whose bodies provoke their own oppression. (Tiffany & Adams, 1985, p. 29)

Tiffany and Adams's (1985) reinterpretation of ethnographic representation reminds us of the hermeneutic circle that is ethnography. It also underlines that within the general allegories of the social science disciplines—the Western cultural stories within which other cultures are framed (Clifford & Marcus, 1986)—there are often allegorical themes woven with the text of gender and gender themes threaded through allegorical ones. Different authors may frame similar situations within different allegories. Likewise, the same allegory may be applied by different authors to very different types of situations. We hear, for example, the voice of a disaffected male who finds a home in the gender-segregated world of the Abelam of Papua New Guinea (Scaglion, 1986). In a male-gendered version of the Edenic allegory, the male anthropologist depicts himself as finding a prefeminist paradise:

> I found the Abelam sexual division of labor quite satisfying personally. . . . I had no moral or ethical problems in assuming an air of sexual superiority consonant with that of the Abelam male. In fact, I am less comfortable with

54

what are for me the redefined sex roles of men and women in the United States, for here I find myself trying to watch my sexism. (Scaglion, 1986, pp. 155-156)

As Back (1993) comments about this statement from the standpoint of 1990s feminist studies of masculinity, "This account is not ambiguous. It clearly shows that for some [Western ethnographers], gender inequality is not on their intellectual, let alone political, agenda" (p. 230).

During the decades of the 1970s and 1980s, a significant amount of feminist work focused on reinterpreting androcentric perspectives and theories. Coming full circle, feminist representation is now itself the subject of re-representation. Women social scientists sometimes find that feminist theories and assumptions are as problematic in understanding women's experience as are androcentric ones. In her analysis of her China notes, for example, Wolf (1990) found the feminist paradigm of the housebound woman-as-victim no more satisfying as an analytic tool than she had the androcentric model. Davis (1986) describes the middle-class feminist bias that she brought to the study of the menopause experiences of Newfoundland women in the 1970s:

My biases were . . . sexist to the extent that I stereotyped the traditional female roles of mother and wife as simple and unsophisticated, chosen only by women because they lacked other opportunities or because they were afraid or incompetent to try anything else. I had entered the field believing that the best representatives of womanhood were those women most like myself, achievers in the public sphere. (pp. 261-262)

Similarly, Deborah Gordon takes to task Southwestern women anthropologists of the 19th and early 20th centuries for their "matronizing" inscription of "Native American women," which she represents as parallel to male patronization of their informants. Matilda Cox Stevenson, for example, during her 1870s fieldwork among the Zuñi, took field notes secretly when her informants objected to her note taking; in a reinterpretation of this activity, Gordon (1993a) writes, "Her zealous salvaging of the Zuni for white consumption permanently damaged her ethnographic relations," and she became a "hurt mother" to the Zuñi (p. 133). The attendance of women at ceremonies where they are "unwelcome" becomes not so much a heroic androgynizing feat as in the 1970s but a form of dominance in the 1990s (Gordon, 1993a, p. 133). Gordon claims that the "gender stories" of the field produced by "matronizing" anthropologists echoed the gender stories found in the general U.S. culture during the late 1930s (economic tales with conflict suppressed), late 1940s (psychiatric categories explaining male-to-female violence), and 1980s (romantic stories, challenges to family mythologies) (Gordon, 1993a, p. 134).

The processes of interpretation and reinterpretation over historical time are evident in three volumes from which we draw some of the material in this monograph. Written in different decades, these works document the changes in the social science discourse of gender over the past 25 years. The first, *Women in the Field: Anthropological Experiences,* edited by Peggy Golde, is a collection of 14 essays by women anthropologists first published in 1970 and republished in 1986. The 1986 edition of the Golde volume includes most of the original material unaltered, with the addition of a preface and a bibliography of later essays and books on sex and gender issues. The second volume is *Self, Sex and Gender in Cross-Cultural Fieldwork,* edited by Tony Larry Whitehead and Mary Ellen Conaway, a collection of 16 essays (6 by men and 10 by women), published in 1986. The Whitehead and Conaway volume takes the Golde volume's generalizations about gender and sex in the field as a discussion point for the analysis made in their introduction and epilogue.

Although several volumes in the social sciences focused on the intersection of gender and fieldwork in the 1990s (Behar & Gordon, 1995; Lamphere et al., 1997; Parezo, 1993b; Pilcher & Coffey, 1996), the volume with most similarities to Golde and to Whitehead and Conaway is *Gendered Fields: Women, Men and Ethnography* (1993), edited by Diane Bell, Pat Caplan, and Wazir Jahan Karim. Canonically for the 1990s in its attention to intersections of gender, ethnicity, and class, this volume is advertised as "international in scope and in the background of its contributors" and as exploring "a cluster of issues [which have] to do with gender and fieldwork from within the framework of recent feminist and postmodern debates."

There are a number of differences of emphasis in the 1970s, 1980s, and 1990s volumes, differences that we think can be understood within the changing historical context of the social sciences. First, the Golde volume is about the experiences of women field-workers; as such, it reflects the first wave of feminist concern with the androcentrism of earlier fieldwork. By contrast, the latter two volumes are by and about women and men in the field, reflecting not only a continuing concern with women's issues but also an awareness of problems and processes in the field related to men and masculinity. Another difference involves the use of theory, with the Whitehead and Conaway volume referencing feminist theoretical per-

56

spectives in a way the Golde volume does not, whereas the Bell volume adds the postmodern to the feminist. Third, both the Whitehead and Conaway and the Bell volumes make more explicit references to the field-worker's own sexual practices and interests than does the Golde volume, which refers to sexuality only in the language of illicit imputations, on one hand, and of licit marital offers, on the other. And finally, there are inter-esting differences in emphasis in the three volumes, particularly the shift in the Bell volume toward a more global-, race-, and ethnicity-informed vision of gender and of anthropological authorship.

Thus, the analysis of ethnographic accountings must itself take into account changes in historical time. Generalizations made during one period of history may not apply during another. The setting, research methods, and disciplinary and personal biography of the field-worker shape the process and productions of fieldwork; all this, in turn, is shaped by history. Analysis in the social sciences is an interpretive rather than an objective process—one that takes place at the intersection of theory, method, discourse, and the historical moment. And gender is one of many themes within that intersection—as feminist theory, as discourse analysis, and as part of the historical self of both the observer and the observed. In all the activities of fieldwork—from the course of one's academic career to entering the field, putting on one's clothes in the morning, writing up field notes, and drafting articles for publication—gender shapes the task. It is inescapable; so our task is to see the shaping through the shapes. But how do we do this?

5.   WARNINGS AND ADVICE

The lack of connection between rapport and rhetoric, between anec-dotes and analysis, is matched by a similar gap between the practical and the epistemological, the methods and the methodology. The methodologi-cal literature divides fairly evenly into practical recipes for action and (sometimes abstruse) philosophical discourses. We think that this great epistemological divide is in part a consequence of fieldwork mythology: the disciplinary tendency to classify experiences in the field according to models, stages, and taken-for-granted categories, such as "role," "entrée," "rapport," "research bargain," and "key informant." These categories, in turn, are either stuffed with anecdotal instances (practical warnings and advice) or scrutinized for epistemological origins (the abstruse phil-osophy). Despite contemporary admonitions to avoid dichotomization

(Bar-On, 1993; Collins, 1991; Fraser, 1989; hooks, 1990; Sprague & Zimmerman, 1993), the tendency to isolate these categories remains, perhaps because of the sheer difficulty of uniting them. In this section, our main concern is the pragmatic, but we do attempt to explore some of the intersections of the practical with the epistemological.

A standard overlapping-stage model of fieldwork is suggested by the methods literature: selecting a topic, the issue of team or lone ranger fieldwork, entrée, trust, rapport, and developing relationships, writing field notes, beginning analysis, developing analysis, writing up findings, and leaving the field. At each of these stages, the gender issues discussed in this volume may be of relevance; it is pragmatic, for example, for the anthropologist to find out something about the clothing and conduct deemed appropriate for women and men in the culture that will be her or his temporary home.

But it would also be useful, in the epistemological long run, to bracket the gender stories we have summarized earlier and to see them as myths bound up with the discourse of fieldwork in the historically grounded fields of academia, rather than as mirrors of interactions in the field. Certain fundamental assumptions underlying social science fieldwork are, we think, gender biased. The 1920s to 1960s language of objectivity in ethnography has given way to a discourse of inclusion (Pollner & Emerson, 1983) or incorporation (Macintyre, 1993), but still the distance remains— the explicit or implicit instruction to the field-worker not to get too close to informants. Mead (1986), the ultimate honorary male anthropologist, cautions against taking on the kind of fictive-kin roles experienced by Jean Briggs as Kapluna daughter on the grounds that such simulated primary relationships draw too heavily on the field-worker's own culture and distort and dim the observers' capacity to maintain the necessary distance that is both warm and limited, affectionate but not passionate, friendly but not partisan (Mead, 1986, p. 324). In Western cultural mythology, as Parezo (1993a) notes, science remains "tough, rigorous, impersonal, competitive, rational, and unemotional," whereas women are "soft, delicate, emotional, noncompetitive, and nurturing" (p. 5).

Gender and Fieldwork Stages

The biographical experiences of women and men provoke varying responses to field sites and research topics. Deep emotional involvement in a setting or issue related to gender or sex can be motivating and productive of strong research interest; this much methodological texts tell us

58

(Lofland & Lofland, 1984). But there may also be issues or settings that arouse feelings of pain, such as Rothman's (1986) work on amniocentesis. Field-workers cannot predict in detail the range and depth of feelings they will come to experience in the field, but often some educated guesses can be made. Warren was asked during the 1980s to get involved in an ethnographic study of protective custody in women's prisons. As in men's prisons, protective custody is used mainly to keep women who have killed or battered their own children from being attacked by other inmates. As a new mother, Warren knew that she would not be able to approach such a setting without distress, so she declined the opportunity. Other times, the emotions can take one by surprise. Hackney's (1995) interview research on women's attitudes toward their bodies had not prepared her for the intensity of emotion expressed in support groups on this topic. She was so distressed by performing participant observation in such an emotive setting that she had to stop attending group meetings and eventually abandoned the research.

Because gender norms within the chosen setting shape the man's or woman's entrée and research relationships, field-workers have to make decisions about the degree to which and the ways in which they will conform to local expectations. As Krieger (1986) notes, gender conformity and deviation in a given culture are processual, dialectical, and reflexive: They change over time, they are related to one another, and they affect not only relationships with respondents but also categories used in interpretation. She adds that gender role expectations in anthropological fieldwork consist of at least four parts:

> 1. distinguishing between what informants are actually communicating about how they expect the anthropologist to behave and what preconceived ideas the anthropologist brings with her or him; 2. distinguishing between what informants expect of one another and what they expect of the anthropologist; 3. distinguishing between aspects of gender role that are crucial and cannot be broken, even by an educated foreigner, and; 4. determining how to break or bend gender expectations to gain the freedom necessary to collect data. (Krieger, 1986, p. 118)

Krieger cautions the field-worker going to a new setting to be as prepared as possible with information about gender roles in the culture but also to remain open to learning about permitted deviance: ways in which norms differ from behavior or norms for foreigners differ from norms for natives. Both her four principles and her discussion of anticipatory and field socialization into gender norms are applicable not only to anthropology but also to sociology, although the norms themselves are not as problematic to sociologists familiar with their own culture. Although a Western woman going to Burma has to be informed that wearing fresh flowers in her hair will be well received, a woman going to the local district attorney's office does not have to be told that this same body adornment will seem slightly strange to the legal natives. Anthropologists learn about gender norms in different cultures by talking to and reading the work of other anthropologists; sociologists learn through their own socialization and status as cultural insiders. Still within the larger (Western) society, there remains a great deal of diversity among groups. What women and men in academic circles find intolerable, acceptable, or required may greatly diverge from notions of appropriateness in other groups within the society. Lack of awareness of norms can impede access, entrée, and relationship formation; thus, the sociologist, like the anthropologist, should strive for awareness of informants' expectations.

Conforming to local gender norms may take personal changes that some social scientists are more and others are less willing to consider. In her discussion of fieldwork in Guatemala, for example, Nancie Gonzalez (1986, p. 92) discusses the problems associated with being a female head of household and a divorced woman. In this Roman Catholic environment, it was her divorced status that eventually posed the most difficulties. Gonzalez notes that if she had to plan the research over again, she would invent widowhood with appropriate rings and photographs to avoid the stigma of divorce. Other social scientists would not be prepared to alter their autobiographies in this manner. Similarly, some anthropological couples are willing to compromise such features of their everyday life (e.g., their division of household labor) in the field site, but others are not (cf. Fleuhr-Lobban & Lobban, 1986; Oboler, 1986).

The practicalities of gender are related not only to lone gun but also to team field research, especially in anthropology. When collaborators share not only research but also households, gender issues can become highlighted. The fieldwork accounts of husband-wife and other cross-gender heterosexual teams in the field indicate both advantages and disadvantages of collaboration. As noted earlier, husband-wife teamwork in the field gives the researcher unique insights into worlds separated by gender (Fleuhr-Lobban & Lobban, 1986; Friedl, 1986; Golde, 1970/1986; Oboler, 1986; Parezo, 1993b). Disadvantages include the strain on a marital relationship that comes with the terrain of fieldwork (Whitehead & Price, 1986) and loss of the unique access afforded the single female researchers by the tendency of people in many cultures to want to adopt them (Whitehead & Price, 1986). In addition, the management of a household, especially if it includes children, can be a burden on the research process, both in the amount of time it takes away from fieldwork and in the refuge it provides from having to make socioemotional connections with informants (Whitehead & Price, 1986).

In the few sociological commentaries on team field research in the 1970s, the "appropriate" gender division of labor was generally taken for granted (Douglas, 1979; Warren & Rasmussen, 1977). This may be due to the fact that, in sociology, the typical research setting was temporally and spatially limited; the field-worker could go back to his or her spouse at night, take research partners of different genders into the field, or go it alone, as circumstances dictate. But at least one published account indicates that for sociologists as well as anthropologists, marriage and other social relationships could become competing commitments to the research endeavor. In the context of changing domestic gender norms in our society—at least among academics—an all-male field-worker team in the 1980s could no longer rely on housewives to take care of domestic routines while they do research. One researcher commented,

> Being married and having family responsibilities, I find usually that I have to go home and attend to those responsibilities. That means that I have difficulty getting notes down quickly, so there's a time lag . . . between the time of my observations and the time I am able to dictate them. . . . I had to come home and be a father to my child and a husband to my wife, and then babysit[19] while my wife went back to work. This certainly interferes with trying to get verbatim quotes down. On the other hand, I am not prepared to sacrifice my family life any more than I already have. (Shaffir, Marshall, & Haas, 1980, p. 60)

Choices must be made not only of what research to engage in but also of what to include or omit in writing up research reports. Issues of gender and sex, as indicated earlier, have been dealt with to varying degrees in varying ways depending on the disciplinary biases in vogue at the moment. From the 1920s until very recently, for example, field-workers were not encouraged to be self-reflexive in their published accounts, avoiding the discussion of emotions in the service of objectivity and the elimination of bias. The topic of sexuality was particularly taboo.

Today, methodological corridor talk encourages the reporting not only of emotions but also of sexual involvements in the field (Whitehead &

Price, 1986). Yet it is not always clear why sexual encounters should be reported, beyond a contemporary confessional impulse. It seems to us that when sexual expectations and encounters are part of the public discourse and when the researcher's participation is analytically salient—for example, in Turnbull's (1986), Styles's (1979), and Wade's (1993) research—then there is seemingly "good reason" to write about it. When the discussion of sexuality illuminates little more than the researcher's personal odysseys, then we think that it may become gratuitous (for a critique of this standpoint, see Wade, 1993). And there are contexts in which the public discussion of sexuality can be damaging to a career in academia. Although there is a public norm of tolerance among social scientists, this may not extend to other disciplines whose university members sit in judgment on such matters as tenure. And the public norm of tolerance is just that: public. Listening to decades of gossip among colleagues has convinced us that whatever it may do for an individual's sense of self, public confession rarely does much for careers.

The Politics of Fieldwork

In their canonical text, *Writing Culture: The Poetics and Politics of Ethnography,* Clifford and Marcus (1986) situate ethnographic work within the fields of language and literature and of political hierarchies and struggles. Those who write and publish ethnography must contend with both.[20] Struggling with the multiple dimensions of the political—including global, national, local, and disciplinary—immerses the ethnographer in a set of debates that involve gender, sexuality, race, ethnicity, and privilege.

Sexism is pervasive in everyday social interactions in the field, in the disciplines, and in other institutions criticized by feminist academics. As we noted earlier, women field-workers may differ in their focus on women and women's issues versus a focus on men. Women in the field also differ in the extent to which they are willing to be confined to gender roles or treated as sexual objects in the pursuit of information (cf. Easterday, Papademas, Schorr, & Valentine, 1977; Warren & Rasmussen, 1977). Women field-workers in male-dominated organizations have reported not only sexual harassment by males but also assignment to traditional female roles and tasks such as mascot, gofer, audience, cheerleader, or the butt of sexual or gender joking (Easterday et al., 1977; Gurney, 1985; Kanter, 1977; Rovner-Piecznik, 1976; Warren, 1972). The female field-worker, like the female professional in a male-dominated organization is a token, and her continued presence in the setting may be contingent upon passing certain loyalty tests, including ignoring derogatory remarks or allowing her gender to provide a source of humor for the group. (Gurney, 1985, p. 44)

Within the current historical context in Western culture, especially within academia, women field-workers can find these roles personally problematic. Ann Fischer (1986) points out that

it is difficult for the American women field worker to adopt a womanly role in a culture in which women are subservient to men. . . . Professional women are not shrinking violets in their own societies, and they are not apt to become so just because the expectation exists in some other culture. (p. 279)

It may be that women refuse to behave as shrinking violets, but there also may be reluctance to publicly admit to such behaviors when they occur. We suspect that the willingness to admit in print to an unprotesting acceptance of sexist treatment is also historically and biographically variable. In Warren's fieldwork, in contrast to her academic life, she did not find the shrinking violet role particularly problematic; indeed, when young, she used to enjoy wearing different masks in the field.[21] Other women, however, have found the sex-gender-knowledge trade-off to be both personally and politically distasteful (Easterday et al., 1977). Despite their discomfort, however, women field-workers may be hesitant to confront informants on the offensiveness of their behaviors (Arendell, 1997; Conaway, 1986; Gurney, 1985). Continued access to the worlds of informants may depend on women field-workers' tolerance of sexist attitudes and actions. As Gurney (1985) notes,

I often wished I were a more militant feminist who could lecture the staff on their chauvinism and insensitivity and change their attitudes toward women. Instead I was always the polite and courteous researcher who tolerated much and said little. I occasionally wondered if I was betraying my beliefs and values, but I allowed it to continue. . . . My tolerance of sexism was based upon my gratitude toward setting members . . . and my concern with maintaining rapport. (p. 56)

Thus, what can be seen, on one hand, as women's "special talent" for field-work can be seen, on the other hand, as a special case of the politics of gender dominance and submission that characterize Western as well as non-Western cultures.

There are a variety of reasons that researchers may be hesitant to publish accounts of gendered or sexualized field relations, and many of the reasons are tied to micro- and macropolitical structures. Reluctance to discuss sex and fear of the consequences to one's own career of describing sexual episodes (Goode, 1999; Gurney, 1985) are two of the reasons that stories of serious sexual hustles remain confined to oral folklore, but they are not the only ones. Women anthropologists have described episodes of unwanted sexual advances from the people they were studying and indicated that they refrained from public discussion of these episodes on grounds of self-blame, gratitude, or political commitments. If the episode occurred in the context of the anthropologist's violation of known local gender codes, then she may believe it was her fault and that she asked for it. In the absence of—or in conjunction with—these feelings, the anthropologist may feel gratitude for the cooperation of the people and an unwillingness to discredit them on this ground but also a more generalized unwillingness to discredit peoples oppressed by colonialism and modernism.[22] Some of the same kinds of political concern have been voiced by sociologists studying racial or social class groups whom they perceive similarly as oppressed; indeed, there is often a general avoidance of reporting any sorts of bad behavior that oppressed or disadvantaged people might engage in, from unwanted sexual advances to drinking and carousing (Whitehead, 1986).

The politics of fieldwork reflects not only a commitment to oppressed peoples but also a lively concern with one's own career as an academic. Such a concern may itself lay the groundwork for the development of gender myths in fieldwork, myths that may reflect more the norms of academia than the culture of the field. During her research in a prosecutor's office, Gurney (1985, p. 45) overlooked incidents that others regarded as sexist because of her discomfort with the idea that her work might have been compromised because of her gender. It was only later that she came to define the problems she had had in the field as related to her gender, rather than other factors such as youth and inexperience. She challenges the rosy view of women as more adept than men at creating and maintaining rapport with respondents in the field. She asserts that being female can result in a lack of credibility in the presentation of research, which in turn promotes concealment of fieldwork problems:

> A female researcher may not discuss the issue of gender in presenting her fieldwork experience for a variety of reasons. . . . [She] may overlook or even deny difficulties she experienced in the field to avoid having her work appear

unsound. Any lapse in rapport with setting members may cast doubt on the information she received from them. There is also the added embarrassment of acknowledging that one's status as a scholar overshadowed one's identity as a female. (Gurney, 1985, p. 44)

Women field-workers live within the field of their disciplines as well as the fields of their ethnographic analysis. Ethnography itself is, to some degree, gendered: The greatest rewards in some social science fields, such as sociology, are given to those who pursue knowledge that is not every-day—it is either highly applied and useful (quantitative gerontology) or extremely theoretical (theory itself). Even in anthropology, in which most practitioners study the everyday, the work of women is often not at the forefront of the disciplinary canon. Parezo (1993b) notes of women an-thropologists of the Southwest,

The . . . scholars presented in this volume have perhaps not been so much hid-den as taken for granted, merging with the shadows like the pines in the forest where the oaks are more prized for their timber. (p. xi)

And, like all other fields, ethnography and the disciplines it occurs within are gendered, sexual, and perhaps sexist fields themselves, with women's contributions and status part of the nexus of disciplinary sexual politics. Women's work in anthropology, according to Parezo, is judged within the context of their private and domestic spheres, from tales of Margaret Mead's (unfeminine) "domineering ways" to corridor talk in which women's ideas are traced to their sleeping with male anthropolo-gists or key informants (Parezo, 1993a, pp. 15-16). Parezo notes that within the field of anthropology, as well as the fields of Tanzania or South London, women are "disciples or fictive daughters in the social hierarchy . . . loyal children and followers in anthropology's oft-feuding families" (Parezo, 1993a, p. 12). As Gordon (1993b) notes, "Anyone who still imag-ines that the university is an ivory tower does not live in it" (p. 430).

Gender and Representation

It is difficult to issue warnings or advice about representation because this is akin to pushing a bus one is riding on. Women writing ethnography must be self-reflexively aware of, attuned to, and familiar with the latest iterations of the representational industry. But despite the undoubted allure of a purely representational stance, the danger is, as Bell (1993) has pointed out, that reality disappears—the event, the person, the emotion, and the gender behind the inscription become, once more, irrelevant. When Denzin (1990) writes of Garfinkel's writing about Agnes, then Agnes herself—the setting, the informant, the field—is lost within a circularity of disciplinary self-representation that has lost the other (see also Clough, 1989). It is important that the other remains in focus as other, in a gendered epistemology and feminist theory (in partial contrast to the more general postmodern). As Margery Wolf (1992) has written of her reading and listening to postmodernists, despite her interest in

> polyvocality, reflexivity, colonialist discourse, audience, the nature of the relationship between anthropologist and informants, and the like—[I am] still . . . just a little more interested in the content of the ethnographies we read and write than in the ethnographers' epistemologies. . . . I see much in the postmodernist ruminations that helps . . . but much also that does not seem to me in the best interests of anthropology at all. (p. 2)

So, bringing together the representational themes of the poetics and politics of ethnography with ethnography itself, our advice to the novice field-worker is to learn to write—to address the concerns raised by Becker (1986) and others. Some of you might even experiment with different forms and strategies of writing: meditative, poetic, or dramatic (see, e.g., Kondo, 1993; Narayan, 1993). We would advise you to take account of the mythological aspects of methodological accounts. And we would advise you to be aware of the self-reflexive aspects of ethnographic representation, from field notes (Emerson, Fretz, & Shaw, 1995; Warren, in press) to published books and articles (Richardson, 1990; Van Maanen, 1988). But, after all, to be a field-worker is to engage in fieldwork, experience incorporation, explore gender in relationships, feel, do, and be.

Warnings and advice, in the last analysis, are pale echoes of fieldwork realities, general principles abstracted from the thick context of research done at other times in other places, by other women and men. Entering the field, developing a place within the social order, and talking, feeling, and living in the setting are the terrain of understanding the intersection of gender, self, and others in fieldwork. Writing field notes, writing articles, using reviews, and engaging in editing are the terrain of understanding the web of data, self, and discourse. The final warning and advice, we think, must be the following: Go into the field, and live, and think, and write. Listen to what we others have said, but do not let our voices become too much the shapers of yours; it is not any researcher who produces a particular ethnography—it is you.

NOTES

1. Grateful thanks to John Van Maanen, Bob Emerson, Nancy Lutkehaus, Bill Staples, Clifford Staples, Barrie Thorne, Constance Ahrons, Peter Manning, and John Johnson for reading the 1988 manuscript. We have retitled this second edition "Ethnography" rather than "Field Research" because the former has become the more common usage in much of the social science literature.

2. Because we are unable, in this short volume, to consider the question of age in any detail, we have omitted a discussion of the ethnography of age and gender in education as represented by sociologists such as Barrie Thorne in the United States and Paul Willis in England.

3. These sections are presented quite disparately; furthermore, the monograph has no concluding section in which the themes we trace are tied neatly together. It is part of the nature of the fieldwork literature, we think, that discussions of practical and epistemological issues and of research relationships and analysis tend to be unconnected. It is beyond the scope of this volume to attempt a grand synthesis. And we suspect that such a synthesis may not be possible; gender, like other concepts, may be framed in a variety of different ways.

4. There are several histories of the Chicago school, including Bulmer (1983), Fine (1995), and Jim Thomas's (1983) excellent special issue of *Urban Life.*

5. We suspect that anthropologists have been more attuned to gender issues in fieldwork than sociologists, at least from the 1920s to the mid-1970s, because gender norms in non-Western cultures are mysterious rather than taken for granted as the social scientist's own.

6. See Warren (1984) for a critique of the concepts (or myths) of trust and rapport in fieldwork.

7. Again, these are the personal characteristics seen as significant in Western culture. It may be that another culture sees as highly significant the length of toes, but the fieldworker might not even discover the other's close—if covert—observation of her or his feet.

8. Achieving a status such as honorary male and access to men's rituals and ceremonies may be facilitated as readily—more readily perhaps—by paying informants in money or goods as by the persevering development of trust and rapport. This principle may be true of numerous sorts of anthropological transactions.

9. It is part of the folklore of contemporary sociology that there is an advantage to both fieldwork and interviewing in minority communities if the researcher is of the same racial and ethnic background as those he or she is studying. This matching theory of rapport is also illustrated by the injunction that women should study women, young people the young, and so on.

10. One exception is if the males in question are gay and so are the bars. Warren was able to do drinking research in the gay male community with little risk of sexual overtures, although they did occasionally occur.

11. We speak here of sexual behavior itself as having no ritual place; reputed sexual involvements (real or imagined) have a highly ritualized place in organizational gossip. And gossip, in turn, is consequential for the conduct of organizational life. Interestingly, Kanter's (1977) book on corporate life, one of the few ethnographies that deals with corporate executive, wives, and secretaries, barely touched on questions of sexual gossip.

12. Warren has learned much about fieldwork methods from the many graduate students in sociology at the University of Southern California and the University of Kansas who have written ethnographies under her supervision. Liz Brunner is one of them.

13. It should also be noted (though we could find no discussions of the issue) that although women and men field-workers can both be victims of violence, they can also both be victims of sexual assault.

14. In Hackney's (1995) research on issues of bodies and social control, sexuality was never the explicit focus; however, in talking about bodies and control, sexuality frequently was discussed. Although she had considered the possibility that interviews might become sexualized, only once did she sense any sexualization of the interview relationship, and that interview occurred with a long-time male friend.

15. Although there is one textbook on field methods from that era (Palmer, 1928), there are few other surviving methodological analyses (Bulmer, 1983, p. 95).

16. It may be that the older the cohort of academic women, the more likely the history of drift. Warren came to this conclusion from conversations with older (e.g., Matilda White Riley in sociology) and younger (e.g., Nancy Lutkehaus in anthropology) cohorts.

17. Examples of this approach include Clifford and Marcus (1986; anthropology), Gusfield (1976; sociology), Stoddart (1986; sociology), and Nicholson (1986; history).

18. In sociology, contemporary concern with text has been not so much with field notes (but see Emerson et al., 1995) but with the ways in which analysis and writing are affected by rhetorical devices (Gusfield, 1976), audiences (Stoddart, 1986; Warren, 1980), interviewee-interviewer gender (Arendell, 1997; DeVault, 1986), and writing technique (Becker, 1986; Richardson, 1990).

19. Despite the language of child care and housework equality in modern professional households, a less egalitarian language reflects a more traditional division of labor. A mother would not describe child care as baby-sitting, the language of outsiders.

20. Here, we focus on the political rather than the literary and technical. However, there are a number of sources to which the novice researcher can turn to improve her or his writing ability (e.g., Becker, 1986; Richardson, 1990).

21. Warren was going to delete the phrase "in her own academic life" as redundant, but then hesitated to do so. She realized that her unwillingness to delete the phrase was a function of her desire not to be seen as totally out of date in the realm of sexual politics (see Hunt's [1984] critique of Warren & Rasmussen's [1977] admission of sexist responses and hiring practices).

22. This summary is taken from comments made by anthropologist colleagues that they did not wish attributed to them.

REFERENCES

Abramson, A. (1993). Between autobiography and method: Being male, seeing myth and the analysis of structures of gender and sexuality in the eastern interior of Fiji. In D. Bell, P. Caplan, & W. J. Karim (Eds.), *Gendered fields: Women, men and ethnography* (pp. 63-77). London: Routledge Kegan Paul.

Adler, P. A., & Adler, P. (1987). *Membership roles in field research*. Newbury Park, CA: Sage.

68

Agar, M. H. (1986). *Speaking of ethnography.* Beverly Hills, CA: Sage.

Allen, C. (1997). Spies like us: When sociologists deceive their subjects. *Lingua Franca, 7,* 31-39.

Amadiume, I. (1993). The mouth that spoke a falsehood will later speak the truth: Going home to the field in eastern Nigeria. In D. Bell, P. Caplan, & W. J. Karim (Eds.), *Gendered fields: Women, men and ethnography* (pp. 182-198). London: Routledge Kegan Paul.

Angrosino, M. V. (1986). Son and lover: The anthropologist as non-threatening male. In T. L Whitehead & M. E. Conaway (Eds.), *Self, sex and gender in cross-cultural fieldwork* (pp. 64-83). Urbana: University of Illinois Press.

Arendell, T. (1997). Reflections on the researcher-researched relationship: A woman interviewing men. *Qualitative Sociology, 20,* 341-368.

Back, L. (1993). Gendered participation: Masculinity and fieldwork in a south London adolescent community. In D. Bell, P. Caplan, & W. J. Karim (Eds.), *Gendered fields: Women, men and ethnography* (pp. 215-233). London: Routledge Kegan Paul.

Bailey, C. A. (1996). *A guide to field research.* Thousand Oaks, CA: Pine Forge.

Bar-On, B.-A. (1993). Marginality and epistemic privilege. In L. Alcoff & E. Potter (Eds.), *Feminist epistemologies* (pp. 83-100). New York: Routledge Kegan Paul.

Becker, H. S. (1986). *Writing for social scientists: How to start and finish your thesis, book or article.* Chicago: University of Chicago Press.

Behar, R. (1995). Introduction: Out of exile. In R. Behar & D. A. Gordon (Eds.), *Women writing culture* (pp. 1-29). Berkeley: University of California Press.

Behar, R., & Gordon, D. A. (Eds.). (1995). *Women writing culture.* Berkeley: University of California Press.

Bell, D. (1993). Introduction 1: The context. In D. Bell, P. Caplan, & W. J. Karim (Eds.), *Gendered fields: Women, men and ethnography* (pp. 1-18). London: Routledge Kegan Paul.

Bell, D., Caplan, P., & Karim, W. J. (Eds.). (1993). *Gendered fields: Women, men and ethnography.* London: Routledge Kegan Paul.

Bendelow, G., & Williams, S. J. (1998). *Emotions in social life: Critical themes and contemporary issues.* New York: Routledge Kegan Paul.

Briggs, J. (1986). Kapluna daughter. In P. Golde (Ed.), *Women in the field: Anthropological experiences* (2nd ed., pp. 19-44). Berkeley: University of California Press.

Bulmer, M. (1983). The methodology of the taxi dance hall: An early account of Chicago ethnography from the 1920s. *Urban Life, 12,* 95-101.

Campbell, M. L. (1998). Institutional ethnography and experience as data. *Qualitative Sociology, 21,* 55-73.

Caplan, P. (1993a). Introduction 2: The volume. In D. Bell, P. Caplan, & W. J. Karim (Eds.), *Gendered fields: Women, men and ethnography* (pp. 19-27). London: Routledge Kegan Paul.

Caplan, P. (1993b). Learning gender: Fieldwork in a Tanzanian coastal village, 1965-85. In D. Bell, P. Caplan, & W. J. Karim (Eds.), *Gendered fields: Women, men and ethnography* (pp. 168-181). London: Routledge Kegan Paul.

Clifford, J. (1986). On ethnographic allegory. In J. Clifford & G. E. Marcus (Eds.), *Writing culture: The poetics and politics of ethnography* (pp. 98-121). Berkeley: University of California Press.

Clifford, J., & Marcus, G. E. (Eds.). (1986). *Writing culture: The poetics and politics of ethnography.* Berkeley: University of California Press.

69

Clough, P. T. (1989). Letters from Pamela: Howard S. Becker's writing(s) for social scientists. *Symbolic Interaction, 12,* 159-170.

Codere, H. (1986). Field work in Rwanda (1959-1960). In P. Golde (Ed.), *Women in the field: Anthropological experiences* (pp. 143-164). Berkeley: University of California Press.

Collins, P. H. (1991). *Black feminist thought: Knowledge consciousness and the politics of empowerment.* New York: Routledge Kegan Paul.

Conaway, M. E. (1986). The pretense of the neutral researcher. In T. L. Whitehead & M. E. Conaway (Eds.), *Self, sex and gender in cross-cultural fieldwork* (pp. 52-63). Urbana: University of Illinois Press.

Cressey, P. G. (1986, April). Comparison of the roles of the "sociological stranger" and the "anonymous stranger" in field research. *Urban Life, 12,* 102-120.

Davidson, J. O., & Layder, D. (1994). *Methods, sex and madness.* London: Routledge Kegan Paul.

Davis, D. (1986). Changing self-image: Studying menopausal women in a Newfoundland fishing village. In T. L. Whitehead & M. E. Conaway (Eds.), *Self, sex and gender in cross-cultural fieldwork* (pp. 240-262). Urbana: University of Illinois Press.

Deegan, M. J. (1995). The second sex and the Chicago school: Women's accounts, knowledge, and work, 1945-1960. In G. A. Fine (Ed.), *A second Chicago school? The development of a postwar American sociology* (pp. 322-364). Chicago: University of Chicago Press.

Denzin, N. K. (1990). Harold and Agnes: A feminist narrative undoing. *Sociological Theory, 8,* 198-216.

DeVault, M. L. (1986, August). *Talking and listening from women's standpoints: Feminist strategies for analyzing interview data.* Paper presented at the annual meetings of the Society for the Study of Symbolic Interaction, New York.

Douglas, J. D. (1979). *Investigative social research: Individual and team field research.* Beverly Hills, CA: Sage.

Douglas, J. D., Rasmussen, P., & Flanagan, C. A. (1977). *The nude beach.* Beverly Hills, CA: Sage.

Easterday, L., Papademas, D., Schorr, L., & Valentine, C. (1977). The making of a female researcher: Role problems in field work. *Urban Life, 6,* 333-348.

Ellis, C. (1995a). Emotional and ethical quagmires in returning to the field. *Journal of Contemporary Ethnography. 24,* 68-99.

Ellis, C. (1995b). *Final negotiations: A story of love, loss and chronic illness.* Philadelphia, PA: Temple University Press.

Emerson, R. M., Fretz, R. I., & Shaw, L. L. (1995). *Writing ethnographic fieldnotes.* Chicago: University of Chicago Press.

Esterberg, K. G. (1997). *Lesbian and bisexual identities: Constructing communities, constructing selves.* Philadelphia, PA: Temple University Press.

Fine, G. A. (1995). *A second Chicago school?* The development of a postwar American sociology. Chicago: University of Chicago Press.

Fischer, A. (1986). Field work in five cultures. In P. Golde (Ed.), *Women in the field: Anthropological experiences* (pp. 267-289). Berkeley: University of California Press.

Fleuhr-Lobban, C., & Lobban, R. C. (1986). Families, gender and methodology in the Sudan. In T. L. Whitehead & M. E. Conaway (Eds.), *Self, sex and gender in cross-cultural fieldwork* (pp. 152-195). Urbana: University of Illinois Press.

Foucault, M. (1978). *The history of sexuality: Introduction.* New York: Pantheon.

Foucault, M. (1980). *Power/knowledge.* New York: Pantheon.

70

Fraser, N. (1989). *Unruly practices: Power, discourse and gender in contemporary social theory.* Minneapolis: University of Minnesota Press.

Freedman, D. (1986). Wife widow, woman: Roles of an anthropologist in a Transylvanian village. In P. Golde (Ed.), *Women in the field: Anthropological experiences* (pp. 335-358). Berkeley: University of California Press.

Freeman, D. (1983). *Margaret Mead in Samoa: The making and unmaking of an anthropological myth.* Cambridge, MA: Harvard University Press.

Friedl, E. (1980). Field work in a Greek village. In P. Golde (Ed.), *Women in the field: Anthropological experiences* (pp. 195-236). Berkeley: University of California Press.

Gagne, P., Tewksbury, R., & McGaughey, D. (1997). Coming out and crossing over: Identity formation and proclamation in a transgender community. *Gender & Society, 11*(4), 478-508.

Goffman, E. (1961). *Asylums.* Garden City, NY: Anchor.

Golde, P. (Ed.). (1986). *Women in the field: Anthropological experiences.* Berkeley: University of California Press. (Original work published 1970)

Gonzalez, N. (1986). The anthropologist as female head of household. In T. L. Whitehead & M. E. Conaway (Eds.), *Self, sex and gender in cross-cultural fieldwork* (pp. 84-100). Urbana: University of Illinois Press.

Goode, E. (1999). Sex with informants as deviant behavior: An account and commentary. *Deviant Behavior, 20*(4), 301-324.

Gordon, D. (1993a). Among women: Gender and ethnographic authority of the Southwest. In N. J. Parezo (Ed.), *Hidden scholars: Women anthropologists and the Native American Southwest* (pp. 129-145). Albuquerque: University of New Mexico Press.

Gordon, D. A. (1993b). Conclusion: Culture writing women: Inscribing feminist anthropology. In R. Behar & D. A. Gordon (Eds.), *Women writing culture* (pp. 430-431). Berkeley: University of California Press.

Gurney, J. N. (1985). Not one of the guys: The female researcher in a male-dominated setting. *Qualitative Sociology, 8,* 42-62.

Gusfield, J. (1976). The literary rhetoric of science: Comedy and pathos in drinking driver research. *American Sociological Review, 41,* 16-34.

Hackney, J. (1995, April). *Sick, bad, wrong and not OK: Women's attitudes towards their body size and eating habits.* Paper presented at the annual meeting of the Midwest Sociological Society, Chicago.

Hackney, J. (1996a, August). *The ideal point of penality: A Foucaultian interpretation of the twelve step movement.* Paper presented at the annual meeting of the Midwest Sociological Society, Chicago.

Hackney, J. (1996b, April). *Stairway to heaven: Religious expressions in an overeaters anonymous group.* Paper presented at the annual meeting of the American Sociological Association, New York.

Hackney, J. (1998, April). *Boundaries built and broken: A descriptive analysis of smoking and social behavior at work.* Paper presented at the annual meeting of the Midwest Sociological Society, Kansas City, MO.

Harkess, S., & Warren, C. A. B. (1993). The social relations of intensive interviewing. *Sociological Methods and Research, 21,* 317-339.

Hertz, R. (1996). Guarding against women? Responses of military men and their wives to gender integration. *Journal of Contemporary Ethnography, 25,* 251-284.

Hochschild, A. R. (1983). *The managed heart: The commercialization of human feeling.* Berkeley: University of California Press.

Holstein, J. A., & Gubrium, J. F. (1995). *The active interview.* Thousand Oaks, CA: Sage.

hooks, b. (1990). *Yearning: Race gender and cultural politics.* Boston: South End.

Hopper, C. B., & Moore, J. (1990). Women in outlaw motorcycle gangs. *Journal of Contemporary Ethnography, 4,* 363-387.

Humphreys, L. (1979). *Tearoom trade: Impersonal sex in public places* (Enlarged ed.). Chicago: Aldine.

Hunt, J. (1984). The development of rapport through the negotiation of gender in field work among police. *Human Organization, 43,* 283-296.

Hutheesing, O. K. (1993). Facework of a female elder in a Lisu field, Thailand. In D. Bell, P. Caplan, & W. J. Karim (Eds.), *Gendered fields: Women, men and ethnography* (pp. 93-102). London: Routledge Kegan Paul.

Jackson, J. (1986). On trying to be an Amazon. In T. L. Whitehead & M. E. Conaway (Eds.), *Self, sex and gender in cross-cultural fieldwork* (pp. 263-274). Urbana: University of Illinois Press.

Johnson, J. M. (1975). *Doing field research.* London: Free Press.

Johnson, N. B. (1986). Ethnographic research and rites of incorporation: A sex- and gender-based comparison. In T. L. Whitehead & M. E. Conaway (Eds.), *Self, sex and gender in cross-cultural fieldwork* (pp. 164-181). Urbana: University of Illinois Press.

Kanter, R. M. (1977). *Men and women of the corporation.* New York: Basic Books.

Karim, W. J. (1993). With "moyang melur" in Carey Island: More endangered, more engendered. In D. Bell, P. Caplan, & W. J. Karim (Eds.), *Gendered fields: Women, men and ethnography* (pp. 78-92). London: Routledge Kegan Paul.

Keller, E. F. (1985). *Reflections on gender and science.* New Haven, CT: Yale University Press.

Kneeland, T., & Warren, C. A. B. (in press). *Pushbutton psychiatry: A history of electroconvulsive therapy in America.* New York: Greenwood.

Kondo, D. (1993). Bad girls: Theater, women of color, and the politics of representation. In R. Behar & D. A. Gordon (Eds.), *Women writing culture* (pp. 48-64). Berkeley: University of California Press.

Krieger, L. (1986). Negotiating gender role expectations in Cairo. In T. L. Whitehead & M. E. Conaway (Eds.), *Self, sex and gender in cross-cultural fieldwork* (pp. 117-128). Urbana: University of Illinois Press.

Lamphere, L., Ragone, H., & Zavella, P. (1997). *Situated lives: Gender and culture in everyday life.* New York: Routledge Kegan Paul.

Landes, R. (1986). A woman anthropologist in Brazil. In P. Golde (Ed.), *Women in the field: Anthropological experiences* (pp. 119-139). Berkeley: University of California Press.

Lederman, R. (1986). The return of redwoman: Fieldwork in highland New Guinea. In P. Golde (Ed.), *Women in the field: Anthropological experiences* (pp. 361-388). Berkeley: University of California Press.

Lofland, J., & Lofland, L. (1984). *Analyzing social settings: A guide to qualitative observations and research.* Belmont, CA: Wadsworth.

Lopata, H. Z. (1995). Postscript. In G. A. Fine (Ed.), *A second Chicago school? The development of a postwar American sociology* (pp. 365-386). Chicago: University of Chicago Press.

Lutkehaus, N. (1982). Ambivalence, ambiguity and the reproduction of gender hierarchy in Manam society, 1933-1979. *Social Analysis, 12,* 36-93.

Lutkehaus, N. (1990). Refractions of reality: On the use of other ethnographers' fieldnotes. In R. Sanjek (Ed.), *Fieldnotes: The making of anthropology* (pp. 303-324). Ithaca, NY: Cornell University Press.

Macintyre, M. (1993). Fictive kinship or mistaken identity? Fieldwork on Tubetube Island, Papua New Guinea. In D. Bell, P. Caplan, & W. J. Karim (Eds.), *Gendered fields: Women, men and ethnography* (pp. 44-62). London: Routledge Kegan Paul.

Mead, M. (1923). *Coming of age in Samoa.* New York: Morrow.

Mead, M. (1986). Field work in Pacific islands, 1925-1967. In P. Golde (Ed.), *Women in the field: Anthropological experiences* (pp. 293-331). Berkeley: University of California Press.

Myers, J. (1992). Nonmainstream body modification: Genital piercing, branding, burning, and cutting. *Journal of Contemporary Ethnography, 3,* 267-306.

Nader, L. (1986). From anguish to exultation. In P. Golde (Ed.), *Women in the field: Anthropological experiences* (pp. 97-116). Berkeley: University of California Press.

Narayan, K. (1993). Participant observation. In R. Behar & D. A. Gordon (Eds.), *Women writing culture* (pp. 34-48). Berkeley: University of California Press.

Nicholson, L. J. (1986). *Gender and history: The limits of social theory in the age of the family.* New York: Columbia University Press.

Oakley, A. (1981). Interviewing women: A contradiction in terms. In H. Roberts (Ed.), *Doing feminist research* (pp. 30-61). London: Routledge Kegan Paul.

Oboler, R. S. (1986). For better or worse: Anthropologists and husbands in the field. In T. L. Whitehead & M. E. Conaway (Eds.), *Self, sex and gender in cross-cultural fieldwork* (pp. 28-51). Urbana: University of Illinois Press.

O'Brien, M. (1989). *Reproducing the world: Essays in feminist theory.* Boulder, CO: Westview.

Palmer, V. M. (1928). *Field studies in sociology: A student's manual.* Chicago: University of Chicago Press.

Parezo, N. J. (1993a). Anthropology: The welcoming science. In N. J. Parezo (Ed.), *Hidden scholars: Women anthropologists and the Native American Southwest* (pp. 3-37). Albuquerque: University of New Mexico Press.

Parezo, N. J. (1993b). Preface. In N. J. Parezo (Ed.), *Hidden scholars: Women anthropologists and the Native American Southwest* (pp. xi-xix). Albuquerque: University of New Mexico Press.

Pilcher, J., & Coffey, A. (1996). *Gender and qualitative research.* Alderschot, England: Averbury.

Pollner, M., & Emerson, R. M. (1983). The dynamics of inclusion and distance in fieldwork relations. In R. M. Emerson (Ed.), *Contemporary field research* (pp. 235-252). Prospect Heights, IL: Waveland.

Richardson, L. (1990). *Writing strategies.* Newbury Park, CA: Sage.

Rothman, B. K. (1986). Reflections: On hard work. *Qualitative Sociology, 9,* 48-53.

Rovner-Piecznik, R. (1976). Another kind of education: Researching urban justice. In M. P. Golden (Ed.), *The research experience* (pp. 465-473). Itasca, IL: R. E. Peacock.

Sass, L. (1986, May). Anthropology's native problems: Revisionism in the field. *Harpers Magazine,* pp. 49-57.

Scaglion, R. (1986). Sexual segregation and ritual pollution in Abelam society. In T. L. Whitehead & M. E. Conaway (Eds.), *Self, sex and gender in cross-cultural fieldwork* (pp. 151-163). Urbana: University of Illinois Press.

Shaffir, W., Marshall, V., & Haas, J. (1980). Competing commitments: Unanticipated problems of field research. *Qualitative Sociology, 2,* 56-71.

Simmel, G. (1950). *The sociology of George Simmel* (Trans., K. H. Wolff). New York: Free Press.

Smith, R. J. (1990). Hearing voices, joining the chorus: Appropriating someone else's fieldnotes. In R. Sanjek (Ed.), *Fieldnotes: The making of anthropology* (pp. 356-370). Ithaca, NY: Cornell University Press.

Sprague, J. (1993, August). *Holy men and big guns: The can(n)on in social theory.* Paper presented at the 88th annual meeting of the American Sociological Association, Miami, FL.

Sprague, J., & Zimmerman, M. K. (1993). Overcoming dualisms: A feminist agenda for sociological methodology. In P. England (Ed.), *Theory on gender/feminism on theory* (pp. 255-280). New York: Aldine.

Stoddart, K. (1986). The presentation of everyday life: Some textual strategies for "adequate ethnography." *Urban Life, 15,* 103-121.

Strathern, M. (1984, July). *Dislodging a world view: Challenge and counter-challenge in the relationship between feminism and anthropology.* Paper presented at the Research Center for Women's Studies, University of Adelaide, Australia.

Styles, J. (1979). Insider/outsider: Researching gay baths. *Urban Life, 2,* 135-152.

Sudarkasa, N. (1986). In a world of women: Field work in a Yoruba community. In P. Golde (Ed.), *Women in the field: Anthropological experiences* (pp. 167-191). Berkeley: University of California Press.

Thomas, J. (1983). Toward a critical ethnography: A reexamination of the Chicago legacy. *Urban Life, 11,* 477-490.

Thorne, B. (1983). *Gender play: Girls and boys in school.* New Brunswick, NJ: Rutgers University Press.

Tiffany, S. W., & Adams, K. J. (1985). *The wild woman: An inquiry into the anthropology of an idea.* Cambridge, MA: Schenkman.

Turnbull, C. M. (1986). Sex and gender: The role of subjectivity in field research. In T. L. Whitehead & M. E. Conaway (Eds.), *Self, sex and gender in cross-cultural fieldwork* (pp. 17-27). Urbana: University of Illinois Press.

Van Maanen, J. (1988). *Tales of the field: On writing ethnography.* Chicago: University of Chicago Press.

Vera-Sanso, P. (1993). Perception, east and west: A Madras encounter. In D. Bell, P. Caplan, & W. J. Karim (Eds.), *Gendered fields: Women, men and ethnography* (pp. 159-167). London: Routledge Kegan Paul.

Vogler, R. J. M. (1993). *The medicalization of eating: Social control in and eating disorders clinic.* Greenwich, CT: JAI.

Wade, P. (1993). Sexuality and masculinity in fieldwork among Columbian Blacks. In In D. Bell, P. Caplan, & W. J. Karim (Eds.), *Gendered fields: Women, men and ethnography* (pp. 199-214). London: Routledge Kegan Paul.

Warren, C. A. B. (1972). *Identity and community in the gay world.* New York: Wiley Interscience.

Warren, C. A. B. (1980). Data presentation and the audience: Responses, ethics, and effects. *Urban Life, 3,* 282-308.

Warren, C. A. B. (1982). *The court of last resort: Mental illness and the law.* Chicago: University of Chicago Press.

Warren, C. A. B. (1984). Toward a co-optive model of qualitative research. *Communication Quarterly, 2,* 104-112.

Warren, C. A. B. (1987). *Madwives: Schizophrenic women in the 1950s.* New Brunswick, NJ: Rutgers University Press.

Warren, C. A. B. (in press). Writing the other, inscribing the self. *Qualitative Sociology.*

Warren, C. A. B., & Rasmussen, P. K. (1977). Sex and gender in fieldwork research. *Urban Life, 6,* 359-369.

Wax, R. H. (1979). Gender and age in fieldwork and fieldwork education: No good thing is done by any man alone. *Social Problems, 26,* 509-522.

Wedgwood, C. (1957). The education of women and girls in the Pacific. *South Pacific, 9,* 495-501.

Weidman, H. H. (1986). On ambivalence in the field. In P. Golde (Ed.), *Women in the field: Anthropological experiences* (pp. 239-263). Berkeley: University of California Press.

Whitehead, T. L. (1986). Breakdown, resolution and coherence: The fieldwork experiences of a big, brown pretty-talking man in a West Indian community. In T. L. Whitehead & M. E. Conaway (Eds.), *Self, sex and gender in cross-cultural fieldwork* (pp. 213-239). Urbana: University of Illinois Press.

Whitehead, T. L., & Conaway, M. E. (Eds.). (1986). *Self, sex and gender in cross-cultural fieldwork.* Urbana: University of Illinois Press.

Whitehead, T. L., & Price, L. (1986). Summary: Sex and the fieldwork experience. In T. L. Whitehead & M. E. Conaway (Eds.), *Self, sex and gender in cross-cultural fieldwork* (pp. 289-304). Urbana: University of Illinois Press.

Williams, T., Dunlap, E., Johnson, B. D., & Hamid, A. (1992). Personal safety in dangerous places. *Journal of Contemporary Ethnography, 3,* 343-374.

Wolf, M. (1990). Chinanotes: Engendering anthropology. In R. Sanjek (Ed.), *Fieldnotes: The making of anthropology* (p. 74). Ithaca, NY: Cornell University Press.

Wolf, M. (1992). *A thrice-told tale: Feminism, postmodernism, and ethnographic responsibility.* Stanford, CA: Stanford University Press.

Yount, K. R. (1991). Ladies, flirts, and tomboys: Strategies for managing sexual harassment in an underground coal mine. *Journal of Contemporary Ethnography, 4,* 396-422.

ABOUT THE AUTHORS

Carol A. B. Warren is Professor of Sociology in the Department of Sociology at the University of Kansas. Her research interests include gender and social control, ethnographic methods, and the history of aging. She is the author of *Madwives: Schizophrenic Women in the 1950s* (1987), *The Court of Last Resort: Mental Illness and the Law* (1982), and, with Timothy Kneeland, *Push-Button Psychiatry: A History of Electroconvulsive Therapy in America* (forthcoming).

Jennifer Kay Hackney is a Ph.D. candidate in the Department of Sociology at the University of Kansas. Her research interests include sociology of the body, medical sociology, gender, social control, and research methodology.

Qualitative Research Methods

Series Editor
JOHN VAN MAANEN
Massachusetts Institute of Technology

Associate Editors:
Peter K. Manning, *Michigan State University*
& Marc L. Miller, *University of Washington*

Other volumes in this series listed on outside back cover